Messiah's Calendar
Book 1

Days, Weeks, Months and Years

An Introduction to Biblical Timekeeping

Messiah's Calendar
Book 1

Days, Weeks, Months and Years

An Introduction to Biblical Timekeeping

James T. and Lisa M. Cummins

Open my eyes, that I may see wondrous things out of Your law.

Psalm 119:18

And God said, "Let there be lights in the firmament of the heaven to divide the day from the night; and let them be for signs, and for seasons, and for days, and years..."

Genesis 1:14

Jerusalem, old city walls and sky with full moon, photo by DYKT Mohigan.

Shofar. Sabbath Horn. Yemenite Jew. Between 1934 and 1939. Matson Photo Service, photographer. G. Eric and Edith Matson Photograph Collection, Library of Congress, Prints and Photographs Division, Washington, D.C. 20540 USA

So teach us to number our days,
that we may apply our hearts unto wisdom.

Introduction

Every event in the Bible is established within God's system of timekeeping. However, own modern calendar is quite foreign to that of the Bible. Not only are the Biblical *months* different from those we use today, but even the definition of a Biblical *day* is not the same as our modern definition.

It is a common misconception that the Jewish people invented their own calendar, infused it into their culture, and finally represented it within the Hebrew scriptures as they recorded the Bible. Actually, the reverse is true. God is the one who instituted the concept of the *day*, ordered the days of the *week*, set down the *months* of the year, and created the special *appointed times*. In His scriptures, we see evidence of the many times that God instructed certain people about His calendar and commanded them to observe it – a calendar which was largely unknown to them. *After* these people agreed to observe God's timekeeping system – predominately the Jewish people – God's calendar *then* became infused into their culture, and there it remains to this day.

This book, *Messiah's Calendar,* is intended to give you ample opportunities to carefully study the key scriptures which speak about God's creation of Biblical timekeeping. It will quickly become evident to you that God, and God alone, is the inventor and first promoter of this system.

If God says His system of timekeeping is important, then – as believers – we wholeheartedly agree. However, since our daily lives are immersed in a modern culture that ignores scriptural principles in general (not to mention a scriptural calendar), it becomes an uphill struggle for us just to *learn* about God's unique way of marking time. That's the purpose of this book... to make it *easy.*

Learning about the Biblical system of timekeeping will open the scriptures to you in a powerful new way. As you study, you will begin to notice that *all* major events and prophecies in the Bible – including those of the New Testament – are anchored in the Biblical calendar system. Once you gain some knowledge of the basics of Biblical timekeeping, you will begin to perceive scripture's divine, built-in "cross-referencing" system which *automatically* connects calendar dates with the events which occurred on those dates – *and* their prophetic significance. Biblical events which used to seem "random" will suddenly "snap into alignment" as you discover their position on His calendar. Each event's place in God's omnipotent plan will become unmistakably clear!

Are you ready to begin? Let's start with a word of thanks to our LORD, Jesus the Messiah, and ask for His help in understanding His calendar. He *wants* to teach it to us. After all... He invented it!

"Lord Jesus, thank You for Your scriptures. Please teach us Your system of timekeeping. We bless Your holy Name. Amen."

> *"For My thoughts are not your thoughts, neither are your ways My ways," says the LORD.*
>
> *Isaiah 55:8*

The day is Thine, the night also is Thine: Thou hast prepared the light and the sun.

Psalm 74:16

The Biblical Day

God keeps time very differently than our modern society does today. The most fundamental difference lies in the Bible's definition of the *day*.

The Biblical day begins at sundown. God first established the definition of a *day* using a specific phrase repeated throughout Genesis chapter 1: *"and the evening and the morning were..."* Six times, He repeated this phrase.

> *And the evening and the morning were* one day. (Gen. 1:5)
>
> *And the evening and the morning were* the second day. (Gen. 1:8)
>
> *And the evening and the morning were* the third day. (Gen. 1:13)
>
> *And the evening and the morning were* the fourth day. (Gen. 1:19)
>
> *And the evening and the morning were* the fifth day. (Gen. 1:23)
>
> *And the evening and the morning were* the sixth day. (Gen. 1:31)

Whenever God repeats a particular word or phrase in scripture, we can be sure that it carries special importance. Here, He was establishing a pattern which would form the entire basis of His timekeeping system: God's definition of the *day*, which begins at *evening* when the sun goes down.

Scriptures defining the Biblical day

Where else in scripture does this definition of the *day* appear? Can it, perhaps, even be found in the New Testament? Let's find out!

A scripture defining the beginning and end of a series of days is in Exodus:

> In the first month, on the fourteenth day of the month *at evening*, you shall eat unleavened bread, until the twenty-first day of the month *at evening*. (Ex. 12:18)

And God called the light Day, and the darkness He called Night. And the evening and the morning were one day.

Genesis 1:5

The Conclusion of the Sabbath, Moritz Daniel Oppenheim, December 31, 1865. This painting depicts a traditional Jewish ceremony known as *Havdalah*, a Hebrew word meaning "separation." Havdalah is held at *nightfall* at the conclusion of every Sabbath or special day of rest. The intent is to mark the ending of the holy day (taking opportunity to thank God for it) and to recognize the day's "separateness" from the ordinary days of the week. Havdalah has been celebrated since before New Testament times and continues to be celebrated today in observant households. Some Bible scholars think that the late night gathering of believers "on the first day of the week" (at which Paul continued speaking until midnight) may have been an extended Havdalah celebration, which would have begun at nightfall at the close of the Sabbath (Acts 20:7-12).

A special day of rest, the *Sabbath*, is mentioned frequently in scripture. There is a weekly Sabbath (the seventh day), but there are also annual "special" Sabbaths which don't necessarily fall on the seventh day. Verses concerning the **beginning of Sabbath days** provide further evidence that God defines a *day* as beginning at *evening*.

> In the ninth day of the month *at evening, from evening to evening,* you shall keep your Sabbath. (Lev. 23:32)

> And it came to pass that, *when the gates of Jerusalem began to be dark before the Sabbath,* I commanded that the doors should be shut... (Neh. 13:19)

New Testament evidence

In the New Testament, we find evidence that God's definition of the Biblical day continued to be honored. For example, Mark chapter 1 relates how the crowds of people brought sick and demon-possessed people to Jesus. They brought their ailing friends and relatives *after sunset,* because they wanted to wait until the Sabbath had *concluded.*

> And at *evening, when the sun had set,* they brought to him all that were diseased, and them that were possessed with demons. (Mk. 1:32; read the full context, Mk. 1:21-34)

The scriptures describe Joseph of Arimathaea coming to Pontius Pilate to ask for Jesus' body at the start of the Preparation Day (the day before a special annual Sabbath). Joseph came as soon as possible on Preparation Day so that he could avoid doing any work on the upcoming Sabbath; scripture says he came in the *evening.*

> When *evening* had now come, because it was the Preparation Day, that is, the day before the Sabbath, Joseph of Arimathaea, a prominent council member who also himself was looking for the Kingdom of God, came. He boldly went in to Pilate, and asked for Jesus' body (Mk. 15:42-46; compare Mat. 27:57-60).

**12:00 am –
The western
day begins**

**Evening –
The Biblical
day begins**

**Evening –
Another
Biblical
day begins**

Comparing the Biblical definition to the western definition

Throughout this book, we will use the terms *western culture, western civilization, western calendar* and *western timekeeping.* In these contexts, the term *western* is intended to mean "of or pertaining to the modern culture of Europe, North America, and other countries of similar culture." For example, the familiar calendar we use in our day-to-day lives for work and school called the *Gregorian calendar* (the one which begins with the month January and ends with the month December), is also referred to as the *western calendar.*

According to western timekeeping, the day begins at 12:00 am (midnight). On the diagram above, the beginning of the western day is indicated.

According to Biblical timekeeping, the day begins at evening. The beginnings of two separate Biblical days are indicated on the diagram.

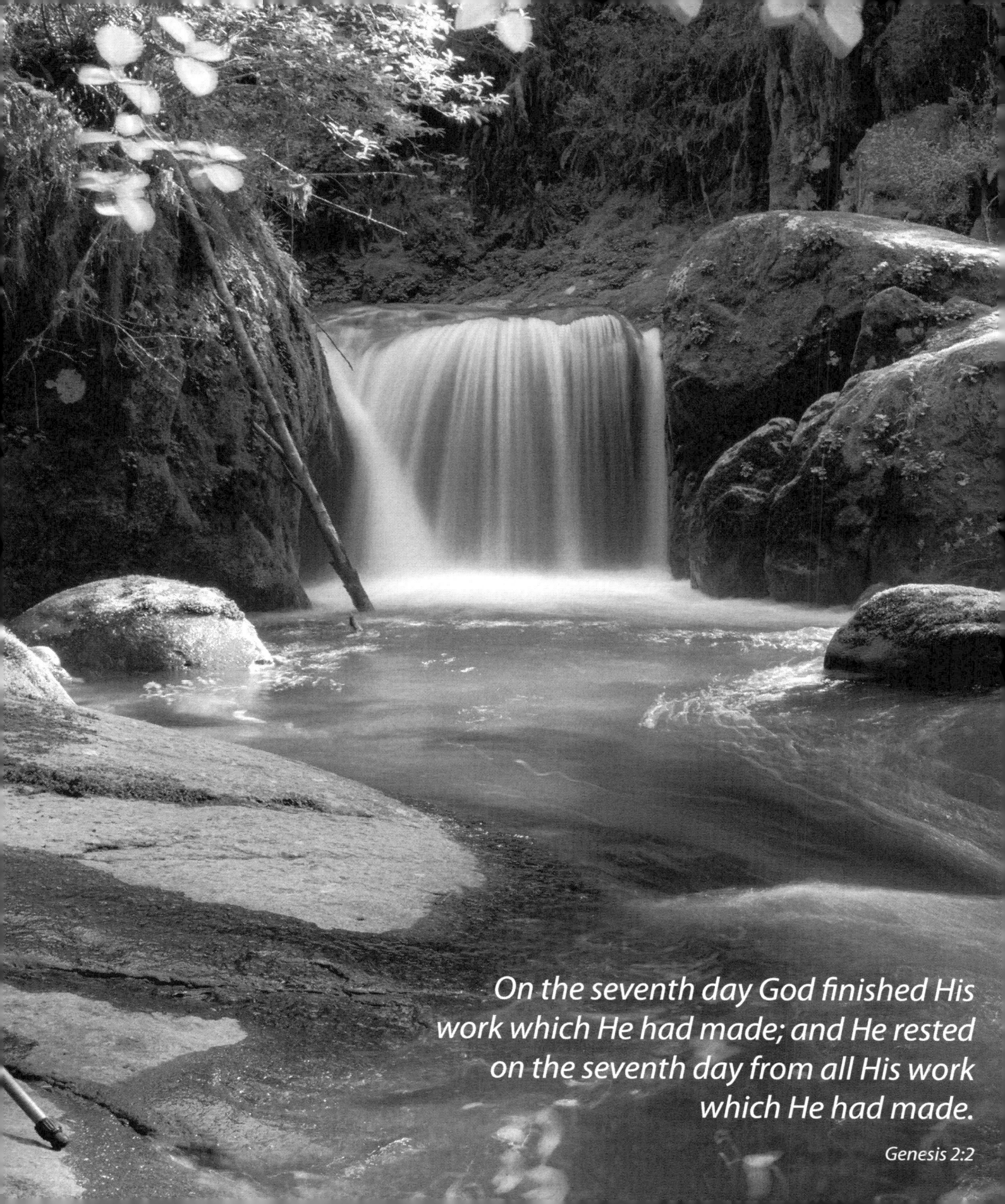

On the seventh day God finished His work which He had made; and He rested on the seventh day from all His work which He had made.

Genesis 2:2

The Biblical Week

In the last section, you learned that the Biblical day is defined quite differently from the western day. In the next section, you will discover that the Biblical week is (thankfully) exactly the same as our western week, except that it uses different names for the days.

About Hebrew and Greek used in this book

Before we go any further, we need to stop right here and reassure you about any Hebrew or Greek words you might come across in this book. As you gradually learn how to locate certain days, months and seasons in your Bible, it will become important to start referring to them using their original Hebrew or Greek names. We realize that most of our readers have never seen Hebrew or Greek letters, so we would never expect you to learn to recognize any of these words in their original languages. Therefore, whenever we present a new Hebrew or Greek word that you really need to know, we will always provide its *pronunciation* (called a *transliteration*) – spelling it out with the letters you use in everyday English.

On the topic of Hebrew... we recognize that our readers come from diverse backgrounds... for example, some are Jews, some are Gentiles. This is one reason why this book alternately refers to our Messiah as either *Jesus* or *Yeshua*. *Jesus* is just the English translation of the good, old-fashioned Hebrew name *Yeshua*. *Yeshua* is the name He was actually called during His time on earth. Either name is accurate and acceptable, one being a translation of the other. In fact, many Messianic believers (like ourselves) tend to use *both* names – Yeshua *and* Jesus – interchangeably in prayer and daily conversation.

Okay... back to the Biblical week!

The days of the Biblical week are *numbered, not named*

The first unique thing you will learn about the Biblical week is that most of the seven days are simply numbered: the *first* day, the *second* day, etc. They don't have special names the way that the western days do. The only exception to this general rule is the *seventh* day. In scripture, it can be referred to as either *the seventh day* or the *Sabbath*. The word Sabbath comes from a Hebrew verb meaning *to rest*. On the next pages, we will provide a graphic that lists the seven days of the week, showing their original Hebrew designations.

> *The days of the Biblical week are referred to by the number of their order in the week.*

Original Hebrew	יוֹם אֶחָד	יוֹם שֵׁנִי	יוֹם שְׁלִישִׁי
Transliteration	yōhm eh-CHAHD	yōhm shay-NEE	yōhm sh'-lee-SHEE
Translation	one day*	second day	third day
Key Verse	Genesis 1:5	Genesis 1:8	Genesis 1:13
Context	*God said, "Let there be light," and there was light. God saw the light, and saw that it was good. God divided the light from the darkness. God called the light "day," and the darkness He called "night." There was evening and there was morning, one day.* *Genesis 1:3-5*	*God said, "Let there be an expanse in the middle of the waters, and let it divide the waters from the waters." God made the expanse, and divided the waters which were under the expanse from the waters which were above the expanse; and it was so. God called the expanse "sky." There was evening and there was morning, a second day.* *Genesis 1:6-8*	*God said, "Let the waters under the sky be gathered together to one place, and let the dry land appear;" and it was so. God called the dry land "earth," and the gathering together of the waters He called "seas." God saw that it was good. God said, "Let the earth put forth grass, herbs yielding seed, and fruit trees bearing fruit after their kind, with its seed in it, on the earth;" and it was so. The earth brought forth grass, herbs yielding seed after their kind, and trees bearing fruit, with its seed in it, after their kind; and God saw that it was good. There was evening and there was morning, a third day.* *Genesis 1:9-13*

Graphic of the days of the Biblical week

The graphic above spans two pages, and is arranged so that you can easily see the original Hebrew name for each day at the top of each column, which is obtained from scripture. Underneath the Hebrew is its pronunciation, or *transliteration*. Throughout this book, you will see the letters *ch* used in our transliterations. They are to be pronounced *ch* as in *Loch Ness* or *Bach*, not *ch* as in *church*. (The Hebrew and Greek languages do not have the sound *ch* as in *church*.) The Hebrew word transliterated *yōhm* means *day*. You may often see it transliterated as *yom*, but this Hebrew word is always pronounced in such a way that it rhymes with *dome* or *roam*, not *mom*.

יוֹם רְבִיעִי

yōhm r'-vee-EE

fourth day

Genesis 1:19

God said, "Let there be lights in the expanse of sky to divide the day from the night; and let them be for signs, and for seasons, and for days and years; and let them be for lights in the expanse of sky to give light on the earth;" and it was so. God made the two great lights: the greater light to rule the day, and the lesser light to rule the night. He also made the stars. God set them in the expanse of sky to give light to the earth, and to rule over the day and over the night, and to divide the light from the darkness. God saw that it was good. There was evening and there was morning, a fourth day.
Genesis 1:14–19

יוֹם חֲמִישִׁי

yōhm chah-mee-SHEE

fifth day

Genesis 1:23

God said, "Let the waters swarm with swarms of living creatures, and let birds fly above the earth in the open expanse of sky." God created the large sea creatures, and every living creature that moves, with which the waters swarmed, after their kind, and every winged bird after its kind. God saw that it was good. God blessed them, saying, "Be fruitful, and multiply, and fill the waters in the seas, and let birds multiply on the earth." There was evening and there was morning, a fifth day.
Genesis 1:20–23

יוֹם שִׁשִּׁי

yōhm shih-SHEE

sixth day

Genesis 1:31

God said, "Let the earth bring forth living creatures after their kind, livestock, creeping things, and animals of the earth after their kind;" and it was so. God made the animals of the earth after their kind, and the livestock after their kind, and everything that creeps on the ground after its kind. God saw that it was good. God said, "Let us make man in our image, after our likeness: and let them have dominion over the fish of the sea, and over the birds of the sky, and over the livestock, and over all the earth, and over every creeping thing that creeps on the earth." God created man in his own image. In God's image He created him; male and female He created them. God blessed them. God said to them, "Be fruitful, multiply, fill the earth, and subdue it. Have dominion over the fish of the sea, over the birds of the sky, and over every living thing that moves on the earth." God said, "Behold, I have given you every herb yielding seed, which is on the surface of all the earth, and every tree, which bears fruit yielding seed. It will be your food. To every animal of the earth, and to every bird of the sky, and to everything that creeps on the earth, in which there is life, I have given every green herb for food;" and it was so. God saw everything that He had made, and, behold, it was very good. There was evening and there was morning, a sixth day.
Genesis 1:24–31

יוֹם שְׁבִיעִי

yōhm sh'-vee-EE

seventh day

Genesis 2:2

The heavens and the earth were finished, and all their vast array. On the seventh day God finished His work which He had made; and He rested on the seventh day from all His work which He had made. God blessed the seventh day, and made it holy, because He rested in it from all His work which He had created and made.
Genesis 2:1–3

This day is also called

שַׁבָּת

shah-BAHT

Sabbath

Exodus 20:11

For in six days the LORD made heaven and earth, the sea, and all that is in them, and rested the seventh day; therefore the LORD blessed the Sabbath day, and made it holy.
Exodus 20:11

*In the Biblical account of creation, the very first day ever created is described literally as "one day" or "Day One," a *unique* description because it was the *only day which had ever existed in the universe as of that time.* Since there had never been any other days among which to place this day in *order,* the Hebrew of Genesis 1:5 does not use the *ordinal* word "first," but rather uses the *cardinal* word "one." In modern daily life, of course, Jewish people now can and do refer to this day of the week as the "first day" (Hebrew יוֹם רִאשׁוֹן *yōhm rih-shōhn).*

How did we get the modern names of the days of the week?

It is usually at this point that students ask a very good question. Since God did not give the days any special names (except for the seventh day), and nowhere in scripture are any special names mentioned, **how did we get the names we use in daily life today?**

Before answering, we must first acknowledge a truth about our world that many of our readers will probably find unsettling. It is certainly not our desire to make you feel uncomfortable, but, as you have probably learned from past experience in reading God's Word, His truth often forces us to admit that "the ways we have always done things" or "the things we always thought were correct" sometimes are inaccurate or even in direct opposition to scripture.

That said, here is one such uncomfortable truth: **Since the western calendar is a worldly system which was designed by wordly empires, most aspects of the western calendar have roots in pagan practices and idolatry.** Throughout history, people who did not worship the God of Bible chose instead to worship the sun, moon, stars, planets, seasons, and the cycles of fertility, birth and death which these heavenly bodies and seasons were believed to govern. Moreover, false gods were associated with these heavenly bodies and events, so that they could be worshipped by name, and entire myths and cultures arose surrounding these spiritual principalities. Annual celebrations were instituted to facilitate idol worship. It should not surprise us that the "god of this world" (Satan) would influence unsaved people to produce a worldwide calendar system that focuses on the names of *his* idols and *their* special days, while attempting to draw humanity's attention *away* from God's Biblical calendar.

The modern names of the days of the week provide an excellent example of the historical pagan influence on our calendar system. On the next page, we list the meanings of the western day names of the English language.

The god of this world has blinded the minds of those who don't believe...

2 Corinthians 4:4

The western names of the days of the week

Sunday (Old English *Sunnandæg*, Latin *dies solis*): "day of the sun"

Monday (Old English *Mōnandæg*, Latin *lunae dies*): "day of the moon"

Tuesday (Old English *Tīwesdæg*, Latin *dies Marti*): "day of Tīw," a god of war and the sky, the equivalent of the Roman god Mars.

Wednesday (Old English *Wōdnesdæg*, from English *Odin*, Latin *Mercurii dies*): "day of Odin," the god Odin or Woden, the equivalent of the Roman god Mercury.

Thursday (Old English *Thunresdæg* or *Thuresdæg*, from Old English *Thunor*, English *Thor*, Late Latin *Jovis dies*): "day of thunder" or "day of Thor" the god of thunder, the equivalent of the Roman god Jupiter (Jovis).

Friday (Old English *Frīgedæg*, from Old English *Frigga*, Late Latin *Veneris dies*): "day of Frigga" the goddess and wife of the god Odin, the goddess of married love – the equivalent of the Roman goddess Venus (Veneris), the goddess of love.

Saturday (Old English *Sæternesdæg*, Latin *Saturni dies*): "day of Saturn," a Roman god.

Occasionally in this book, we will make comparisons between the Biblical calendar and the western calendar, mainly to illustrate the spiritual significance and holiness of God's system of timekeeping in contrast to man's.

We are thankful that, by God's grace, it is possible to be "*in* this world, but not *of* this world." As believers in Yeshua, it is certainly never our intention to honor or celebrate *any* system which has to do with false gods, and our gracious and loving God knows our hearts. Also, He is by no means shocked or surprised by the pagan history of the world's calendar, which has been the case for thousands of years. He understands that we must live within modern society, and this society has imposed its calendar upon our daily lives, like it or not. Even while we use the western calendar every day, it is beneficial to simply be able to hold the facts about it in our hearts. Just knowing how strong an influence it has had on humanity through the centuries can strengthen our spiritual resolve to be "salt and light" in a fallen, corrupt world.

> *"...they are not of the world, even as I am not of the world. I pray not that You would take them from the world, but that You would keep them from the evil one."*
>
> *John 17:14-15, in a prayer said by Yeshua regarding believers*

Days of the week mentioned in scripture

It is extremely beneficial to read about God's system of timekeeping in scripture, because scripture renews our minds and regenerates our thoughts. "Don't be conformed to this world, but be transformed by the renewing of your mind," says Romans 12:2. Below is a selected list of scriptures which illustrate God's designations for the **days of the week.** For the sake of brevity, this is not an exhaustive list; it is merely a representative sample.

It's important to understand the flexibility of these designations. Although both the Old and New Testaments contain many Hebrew and Greek phrases of the terms *the first day, the second day,* etc., they can and do refer to things other than just days of the week. For example, they might indicate the *first day* of a king's reign, the *second day* of the month, or the *third day* that Jonah was in the belly of the great sea creature. In the list below, we were careful to include only places in scripture where the **days of the week** are the intended meaning.

Each verse is shown in its original language, either Hebrew or Greek (with the designation for the day of the week highlighted with a gray box), followed by the English translation.

First day

וַיִּקְרָא אֱלֹהִים לָאוֹר יוֹם, וְלַחֹשֶׁךְ קָרָא לָיְלָה. וַיְהִי עֶרֶב וַיְהִי בֹקֶר, יוֹם אֶחָד.

God called the light "day," and the darkness He called "night." There was evening and there was morning, **one day**. *God creates the first day, Genesis 1:5 Note the unique designation "one day" or "day one."*

Τῇ δὲ μιᾷ τῶν σαββάτων, Μαρία ἡ Μαγδαληνὴ ἔρχεται πρωὶ, σκοτίας ἔτι οὔσης, εἰς τὸ μνημεῖον, καὶ βλέπει τὸν λίθον ἠρμένον ἐκ τοῦ μνημείου.

Now on the **first day of the week**, Mary Magdalene went early, while it was still dark, to the tomb, and saw the stone taken away from the tomb. *Mary discovers the empty tomb, John 20:1*

Ἐν δὲ τῇ μιᾷ τῶν σαββάτων, συνηγμένων ἡμῶν κλάσαι ἄρτον, ὁ Παῦλος διελέγετο αὐτοῖς, μέλλων ἐξιέναι τῇ ἐπαύριον, παρέτεινέν τε τὸν λόγον μέχρι μεσονυκτίου.

On the **first day of the week**, when the disciples were gathered together to break bread, Paul talked with them, intending to depart on the next day, and continued his speech until midnight. *The Jewish believers gather, probably for the traditional meal following the evening Havdalah ceremony of prayers and songs marking the end of the Sabbath (held at nightfall as the first day of the week begins), Acts 20:7*

Second day

וַיִּקְרָא אֱלֹהִים לָרָקִיעַ שָׁמָיִם. וַיְהִי עֶרֶב וַיְהִי בֹקֶר, **יוֹם שֵׁנִי.**

God called the expanse "heaven." There was evening and there was morning, a **second day**. *God creates the second day, Genesis 1:8*

Third day

וַיְהִי עֶרֶב וַיְהִי בֹקֶר, **יוֹם שְׁלִישִׁי.**

There was evening and there was morning, a **third day**. *God creates the third day, Genesis 1:13*

Fourth day

וַיְהִי עֶרֶב וַיְהִי בֹקֶר, **יוֹם רְבִיעִי.**

There was evening and there was morning, a **fourth day**. *God creates the fourth day, Genesis 1:19*

Fifth day

וַיְהִי עֶרֶב וַיְהִי בֹקֶר, **יוֹם חֲמִישִׁי.**

There was evening and there was morning, a **fifth day**. *God creates the fifth day, Genesis 1:23*

Sixth day

וַיַּרְא אֱלֹהִים אֶת כָּל אֲשֶׁר עָשָׂה, וְהִנֵּה, טוֹב מְאֹד.
וַיְהִי עֶרֶב וַיְהִי בֹקֶר, יוֹם הַשִּׁשִּׁי.

God saw everything that He had made, and, behold, it was very good. There was evening and there was morning, a **sixth day**. *God creates the sixth day, Genesis 1:31*

וְהָיָה בַּיּוֹם הַשִּׁשִּׁי וְהֵכִינוּ אֵת אֲשֶׁר יָבִיאוּ, וְהָיָה מִשְׁנֶה עַל
אֲשֶׁר יִלְקְטוּ יוֹם יוֹם.

It shall come to pass on the **sixth day**, that they shall prepare that which they bring in, and it shall be twice as much [manna] as they gather daily. *God commands that the people of Israel gather twice as much manna on the sixth day of the week, so that on the seventh they may rest from gathering, Exodus 16:5*

רְאוּ כִּי יהוה נָתַן לָכֶם הַשַּׁבָּת, עַל כֵּן הוּא נֹתֵן לָכֶם בַּיּוֹם הַשִּׁשִּׁי
לֶחֶם יוֹמָיִם. שְׁבוּ אִישׁ תַּחְתָּיו אַל יֵצֵא אִישׁ מִמְּקֹמוֹ בַּיּוֹם הַשְּׁבִיעִי.

Behold, because the Lord has given you the Sabbath, therefore He gives you on the **sixth day** the bread of two days. Everyone stay in his place. Let no one go out of his place on the seventh day. *God reminds the people of His commandment to rest on the seventh day after some disobey him by going out on the seventh day to gather manna, Exodus 16:29*

Seventh day

וַיְכַל אֱלֹהִים בַּיּוֹם הַשְּׁבִיעִי מְלַאכְתּוֹ אֲשֶׁר עָשָׂה וַיִּשְׁבֹּת בַּיּוֹם הַשְּׁבִיעִי מִכָּל
מְלַאכְתּוֹ אֲשֶׁר עָשָׂה. וַיְבָרֶךְ אֱלֹהִים אֶת יוֹם הַשְּׁבִיעִי וַיְקַדֵּשׁ אֹתוֹ כִּי בוֹ
שָׁבַת מִכָּל מְלַאכְתּוֹ אֲשֶׁר בָּרָא אֱלֹהִים לַעֲשׂוֹת.

On the **seventh day** God finished His work which He had made; and He rested on the **seventh day** from all His work which He had made. God blessed the **seventh day**, and made it holy, because He rested in it from all His work which He had created and made. *God creates the seventh day, rests on it, and makes it a holy day, Genesis 2:2–3*

שֵׁשֶׁת יָמִים תַּעֲשֶׂה מַעֲשֶׂיךָ וּבַיּוֹם הַשְּׁבִיעִי תִּשְׁבֹּת לְמַעַן יָנוּחַ שׁוֹרְךָ וַחֲמֹרֶךָ
וְיִנָּפֵשׁ בֶּן אֲמָתְךָ וְהַגֵּר.

Six days you shall do your work, and on the **seventh day** you shall rest, that your ox and your donkey may have rest, and the son of your handmaid, and the alien may be refreshed. *God commands His people, as well as the animals and foreigners among them, to rest on the seventh day, Exodus 23:12*

בֵּינִי וּבֵין בְּנֵי יִשְׂרָאֵל אוֹת הִוא לְעֹלָם, כִּי שֵׁשֶׁת יָמִים עָשָׂה יהוה
אֶת הַשָּׁמַיִם וְאֶת הָאָרֶץ, וּבַיּוֹם הַשְּׁבִיעִי שָׁבַת וַיִּנָּפַשׁ.

It is a sign between me and the children of Israel forever; for in six days the LORD made heaven and earth, and on the **seventh day** He rested, and was refreshed. *God declares the seventh day to be the eternal sign of His covenant with Israel, Exodus 31:17*

εἴρηκεν γάρ που περὶ τῆς ἑβδόμης οὕτως, Καὶ κατέπαυσεν ὁ θεὸς ἐν τῇ ἡμέρᾳ τῇ ἑβδόμῃ ἀπὸ πάντων τῶν ἔργων αὐτοῦ...

For he has said this somewhere about the **seventh day**, "God rested on the **seventh day** from all His works..." *The writer of Hebrews relates the seventh day rest to the believer's state of rest which he experiences upon receiving forgiveness for sin through the mercy and grace of Yeshua, Hebrews 4:4*

The other name for the seventh day

The other name that God uses for the seventh day of the week is *Sabbath*. If you search for all occurrences of the English word *Sabbath* in your Bible, you will find at least 170 of them. More than 60 of those occurrences are in the New Testament alone.

The reason that the word *Sabbath* is so prevalent in the scriptures is because **it is the fundamental unit in God's system of sanctification of time.** That's right... among other things, God actually *sanctifies time.*

The sanctification of time

Sanctification means "setting something apart or declaring something as holy."

You've read your Bible and seen all the narratives where God sets apart a certain *place* as *holy* or *sanctified* – sometimes it is a piece of land, sometimes the top of a certain mountain, maybe an altar made from a pile of stones, perhaps His tabernacle or His temple. Bible scholars refer to this phenomenon as *sanctification of place.*

What about *sanctification of people?* Now, there's a term that's more familiar to us. Think of the people who have been sanctified – set apart by God – throughout history. There have always been special sanctifications for specific callings, as in the "greats" – Noah, Moses, Elijah, Isaiah, Enoch, Job, Paul, Peter. There is also a sort of *group* sanctification for the purpose of being a light to the nations or salt of the earth – the people of Israel being the primary example, not to mention the thousands of saved Gentiles who spread the good news of salvation throughout the world. Most important of all is the sanctification of the *individual* person, the person who becomes "born again," who has been miraculously "set apart" from this wicked world by our LORD. We, as believers, have been set apart, *sanctified*, through God's salvation – and into His righteousness.

So, should it really surprise us that God also chooses to sanctify *periods of time?* Scripture teaches that He has done so since time itself began! The only reason it may seem startling and new is because of our own unfamiliarity with this particular concept in scripture. It is simply not taught much today. God's sanctification of *people* and *places* is frequently taught and discussed, which is why those two concepts don't feel as strange. However, just talk to any unbeliever who has never set foot in a church or synagogue and never cracked open a Bible, and he will tell you that *all three* sanctification concepts seem weird. Allow yourself to absorb the scriptures presented throughout the remainder of this book, and the Holy Spirit will gently open your eyes to His *sanctification of time.*

Let's not fight about it, okay?

Sabbath is (sadly) one of the most divisive topics among believers today. As we write this book, we find ourselves in the delicate position of needing to teach about Sabbath (because it is foundational to God's calendar), yet desperate to avoid the "baggage" of centuries of denominational dogma and strife which have insinuated themselves, uninvited, into God's holy day.

Instead of talking about the different ways human beings *feel* about the Sabbath and *if* or *how* it ought to be observed, we're going to take the novel approach of simply showing you what the word really means in Hebrew and Greek. Then we will list a few key scriptures in which *God* tells *us* what the Sabbath means to *Him*. And we will leave it at that.

We want to reassure you that **we don't have any particular agenda regarding Sabbath or any part of God's calendar.** In other words, we don't want to "convert you" to any particular belief or lifestyle.

On the subject of God's calendar (or any other subject not essential to salvation), we believe that *no one can dictate to you what to believe, how to live or how to worship.* Jesus Himself prefers to present the truth as an if-then, choice-consequence statement. *If you believe in Me, then I will give you eternal life,* for example. *If you open the door to My knocking, then I will come in.* He never demands robotic, thoughtless submission. Instead, He presents a clear *choice* to each individual, then waits to see what their heart will choose. Will they *choose* to live in the manner He prescribes? Will they *choose* to even believe that His words are true at all? If so, blessings will flow. In the end, God wants *willing* hearts which respond to Him out of love, not a tyranny built on fear and oppression.

Following Yeshua's example in the spirit of gentleness, our approach throughout this book will be based on the fact that *any decision you make regarding studying or observing God's calendar is between two people: you and God.* We trust that our Lord, having brought you miraculously to salvation in the first place, is more than capable of answering all your questions and concerns about matters not essential to salvation, and that includes the Sabbath and all the other elements of His calendar.

The topic of Sabbath is so deep and so vast that it really requires its own dedicated book (or series of books) to fully explore it. It's a wonderful, immense, holy, Godly topic. Once you are finished with this book, we urge you to grab a concordance and chase down every reference to the word "Sabbath" in both Old and New Testaments. Read each one in context. It will be well worth your while. We promise that you will be blessed and refreshed.

> *"Take My yoke upon you, and learn from Me, for I am gentle and lowly in heart; and you will find rest for your souls."*
>
> Matthew 11:29, the words of Jesus

> The Hebrew word for Sabbath carries wonderful meaning in its root letters.

The meaning of the word *Sabbath*

The Hebrew language is built on a system of *roots*. Just as in English and many other languages, *roots* are small chunks of letters (not prefixes or suffixes) which carry a basic meaning. By attaching various other letters around the root letters, the language can produce many new words which are related to the root meaning in some way. The Hebrew word for *Sabbath* carries wonderful meaning in its root letters. Before we look into the Hebrew, though, let's start with an easy example from English.

An example of a root in English

A good example of a root in English is the collection of letters r-e-s-t, *rest*. The basic meaning of this root is *stop, pause, repose, cease from motion or work, sleep, be undisturbed.* How might this root be used in various English words?

> *rest* (verb) - to cease from motion or work, to repose, to stop
>
> *rest* (noun) - a period of repose or quiet
>
> *arrest* (verb) - to cause to stop, to stay, to halt
>
> *arresting* (adjective) - so striking that it brings one to a halt
>
> *restful* (adjective) – having an undisturbed or placid quality
>
> *unrest* (noun) – agitation, disturbance, turmoil, chaos

In the list above, the root's meaning pervades every word. Hebrew roots function in the same manner.

The Hebrew root letters of the word *Sabbath*

Hebrew roots are usually formed by three letters (or sometimes two). In the case of the word *Sabbath*, its Hebrew root letters are the consonants *sheen* שׁ, *bayt* בּ and *tahv* ת. The order of Hebrew letters (and words) is from **right to left.** (By the way, most of those little dots and dashes above and below Hebrew letters are vowel sounds. Vowels are not part of the root, so you should focus on looking at the major letter shapes when studying Hebrew roots.)

On the next page is an enlarged graphic of the Hebrew word for Sabbath, which is pronounced *shah-BAHT.*

The Hebrew word *Sabbath*

pronounced shah–BAHT

שַׁבָּת

Third root letter:
ת *TAHV*

Second root letter:
בּ *BAYT*

First root letter:
שׁ *SHEEN*

Okay... so we know that this word is a noun meaning "Sabbath," but what do its three root letters signify?   These three letters form a primary root which means *to cease, to desist, to rest*.   The root letters are displayed in the box below.

The Hebrew root *rest, cease*

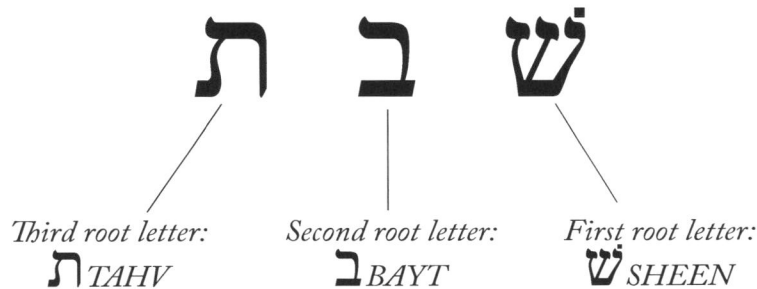

ת   בּ   שׁ

Third root letter:
ת *TAHV*

Second root letter:
בּ *BAYT*

First root letter:
שׁ *SHEEN*

Just as in English, this root is used to form many different words in Hebrew, all related to the basic meaning of *rest, cease, desist*. In the box below is an example of one such word, a verb form in the past tense, meaning "he rested." Notice the identical root letters, as well as the similarity in pronunciation to the noun form Sabbath, *shah-BAHT.*

The Hebrew verb *he rested*

pronounced shah–VAHT

שָׁבַת

Third root letter:
ת *TAHV*

Second root letter:
בּ *BAYT*

First root letter:
שׁ *SHEEN*

Sabbath basically means "a rest"

From the root study on the previous page, it's clear that the noun *Sabbath* actually means *a rest, a ceasing, a period of repose*. This word is often translated *day of rest*, but the Hebrew word for *Sabbath* is used in scripture to refer to other periods of time as well, such as a *sabbath year*.

The definitive text

The definitive text in scripture which connects the Hebrew verb *he rested* with the noun *Sabbath* is Exodus 31:16-17. In this passage, God commands Israel to observe the Sabbath on the grounds that God Himself rested on that day, the seventh day (Ex. 31:17). Further, God determines that the Sabbath is to be the everlasting sign of His covenant with Israel. We have provided the Hebrew text of Exodus 31:16-17 below, and have highlighted in gray the places where the words *Sabbath* and *he rested* appear. Underneath each Hebrew word is the English translation. If you would like to read along in English, remember that Hebrew goes *from right to left,* so **start at the top right of the paragraph.** Try to identify the three root letters that the highlighted words have in common.

וְשָׁמְרוּ בְנֵי יִשְׂרָאֵל אֶת הַשַּׁבָּת לַעֲשׂוֹת אֶת הַשַּׁבָּת לְדֹרֹתָם,

for their generations	*the Sabbath*	–	*to do/observe*	*the Sabbath*	–	*Israel*	*the sons of shall keep*

בְּרִית עוֹלָם. בֵּינִי וּבֵין בְּנֵי יִשְׂרָאֵל אוֹת הִוא לְעֹלָם,

for eternity	*it is*	*a sign*	*Israel*	*the sons of and*	*between Me*	*eternity a covenant of*

כִּי שֵׁשֶׁת יָמִים עָשָׂה יהוה אֶת הַשָּׁמַיִם וְאֶת הָאָרֶץ,

the earth	*and*	*the heaven*	–	*the* LORD	*made*	*days*	*six for*

וּבַיּוֹם הַשְּׁבִיעִי שָׁבַת וַיִּנָּפַשׁ.

and was refreshed	*He rested*	*seventh and on the day*

Therefore the children of Israel shall keep the **Sabbath**, to observe the **Sabbath** throughout their generations, for a perpetual covenant. It is a sign between Me and the children of Israel forever; for in six days the LORD made heaven and earth, and on the seventh day **He rested,** and was refreshed.

It is important to understand the context here. These are the very words of God, commanding Moses to instruct the people exactly how they were to order their daily lives. The seriousness of this instruction is underscored by the Hebrew word "eternity" appearing twice. God claims that the underpinning of the existence of Sabbath is "because He rested on it," (i.e., He invented the entire concept). Within the very order of the Hebrew letters which spell the highlighted words, then, is the truth that God has eternally bound together the two concepts of *His resting on the seventh day* and *His chosen name for that day of rest, the Sabbath.*

Sabbath in the Greek New Testament

What about the meaning of the word Sabbath in Greek? The word for Sabbath in Greek is also eye-opening. It is a noun, the singular form being σάββατον, pronounced *SAH-bah-ton*, and is translated as *Sabbath* or, interestingly, *week*. (The reason it can be translated as *week* is because it was known to be the *seventh* day of the week and therefore acted as the mark of a week's completion, so one could count the number of *Sabbaths* which passed to arrive at the number of complete *weeks* which had passed. The meanings eventually became interchangeable.) Note: Greek words can experience many changes to their suffixes, depending on their grammatical function within a sentence. Therefore, you may see all of these Greek spellings for *Sabbath* in the New Testament: σάββασιν, σάββατα, σαββάτῳ, σαββάτων, σάββατον, or σαββάτου.

Some representative texts

We have selected just a few of the more than 60 scriptures mentioning *Sabbath* in the New Testament, and we have highlighted in gray any occurrences of this word in Greek.

Ἦν δὲ διδάσκων ἐν μιᾷ τῶν συναγωγῶν ἐν τοῖς σάββασιν.

He was teaching in one of the synagogues on the **Sabbath** day. *Jesus habitually taught in the synagogues on the Sabbath day, Luke 13:10*

ὑποστρέψασαι δὲ ἡτοίμασαν ἀρώματα καὶ μύρα. Καὶ τὸ μὲν σάββατον ἡσύχασαν, κατὰ τὴν ἐντολήν.

They returned, and prepared spices and ointments. On the **Sabbath** they rested according to the commandment. *The women who intended to prepare Yeshua's body for burial waited to do so until they had observed the Sabbath, Luke 23:56*

διελέγετο δὲ ἐν τῇ συναγωγῇ κατὰ πᾶν σάββατον, ἔπειθέν τε Ἰουδαίους καὶ Ἕλληνας.

He reasoned in the synagogue every **Sabbath**, and persuaded Jews and Greeks. *Paul discussed the scriptures in the synagogue in Corinth every Sabbath, Acts 18:4*

ἄρα ἀπολείπεται σαββατισμὸς τῷ λαῷ τοῦ θεοῦ·

There remains therefore a **Sabbath** rest for the people of God. *The writer of Hebrews relates the seventh day rest of God (vs. 4) to a spiritual rest from works achieved by entering into God's righteousness by faith, and to a yet future "perfect rest" for believers in the eternal state, Hebrews 4:9.*

*Sound the ram's horn
at the new moon...*

Psalm 81:3

The Biblical Month

The start of every Biblical month was (and, for some, still is) a time for trumpets and worship for observant Jews (and some Gentiles, too). God established the cycles of the moon as the signals for the beginning and end of each month. Therefore, **the Biblical calendar is essentially a lunar calendar.**

In contrast, **our modern western calendar is a solar calendar.** The western calendar bases its 365 days on the position of the earth relative to the sun, then divides the months into 12 periods of time within that 365-day span. For this reason, the months of the Bible almost never align with the months of the western calendar.

The Biblical month begins with a *new moon*

Throughout Bible times, the beginning of every month has always been marked by the appearance of the **new moon**. The ancient definition of the *new moon* was when the smallest "sliver" of a crescent of light first became noticeable at the start of every lunar cycle (see photo at left). Modern astronomers would technically define this as the *waxing crescent*, but in Bible times, this unmistakable crescent was considered to be the sufficient requisite evidence that the *new moon* had indeed occurred. On the next pages, we provide a graphic showing all the phases of the moon throughout a month.

Mentions of the *new moon* in scripture

When scripture speaks of the *new moon*, it is simply referring to *the first day of the month*. The Hebrew phrase for *first of the month* is רֹאשׁ חֹדֶשׁ – literally "head of the month" – pronounced *rōsh CHŌ-desh*. (The word *rōsh* has a long *ō* sound as in *boat*, so *rōsh* rhymes with *gauche* or *cloche*.) Below is a brief list of scriptures which mention the Hebrew phrases *new moon* or *Rosh Chodesh:*

> Blow the ram's horn at the **new moon**... for it is an ordinance of the God of Jacob (Psalm 81:3-4)

> ...on the **first of your months** you shall blow the trumpets... (Num. 10:10)

> From one **new moon** to another...all mankind shall come to worship before Me (Isa. 66:23)

> ...then Solomon offered burnt offerings to the LORD... for the **new moons**... (2 Chron. 8:12-13)

> The people of the land shall worship...before the LORD on the Sabbaths and on the **new moons** (Ezek. 46:3)

Also in the day of your gladness, and in your set feasts, and in the beginnings of your months, you shall blow the trumpets over your burnt offerings, and over the sacrifices of your peace offerings; and they shall be to you for a memorial before your God. I am the LORD your God.

Numbers 10:10

**New moon –
The first day of the
Biblical month
i.e., Rosh Chodesh**

*Ancient definition of a new
moon: the first appearance
of a sliver of a crescent of
light discernable to the
naked eye*

How the new moon was celebrated

From the list of scriptures on the preceding page, there is evidence that Rosh Chodesh / the new moon was an event accompanied by **gladness, feasting, worship** and **sacrifice**, but the Bible doesn't provide all the details. Clearly, Moses at some point passed along God's instruction as to its proper observance regarding the sacrifices for that day:

> On the altar of the LORD that he had built in front of the portico, Solomon sacrificed burnt offerings to the LORD, according to the daily requirement for offerings commanded by Moses for the Sabbaths, the **New Moons** and the three annual festivals... (2 Chron. 8:12-13)

The new moon – scary witchcraft stuff?

In addition to recent movie franchises associating the term "new moon" with vampires and magic, pagan religions have *always* superimposed idolatrous significance upon the phases of the moon, as well as solar events such as equinoxes and solstices. Satan's religions have simply perverted the true holy purpose of astronomical events and signs, which were created by God Himself for His purpose of Biblical timekeeping. God said, "Let there be lights in the firmament of the heaven... and let them be for signs, and for seasons, and for days, and years..." (Gen. 1:14)

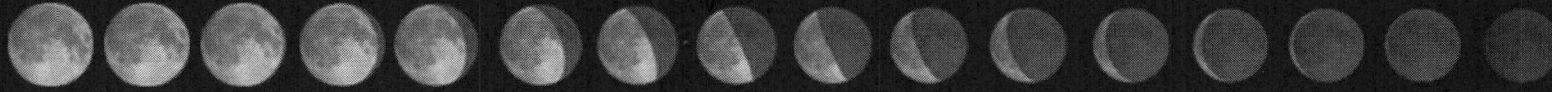

Doesn't God "hate" new moons, though?

Isn't there somewhere in scripture where God says, "I hate your new moons"? Let's read God's actual words in context.

> When you come to appear before Me, who has required this at your hand, to trample My courts? Bring no more vain offerings. Incense is an abomination to Me; **new moons**, Sabbaths, and convocations: I can't bear iniquity along with the evil assembly. My soul hates your **new moons** and your appointed feasts. They are a burden to me. I am weary of bearing them. When you spread forth your hands, I will hide My eyes from you. Yes, when you make many prayers, I will not hear. Your hands are full of blood. Wash yourselves, make yourself clean. Put away the evil of your doings from before My eyes. Cease to do evil. Learn to do well. Seek justice. Relieve the oppressed. Judge the fatherless. Plead for the widow (Isaiah 1:12-17).

The complete context of the chapter is God's exhortation to a people who had become *completely* immersed in, and infested by, sinful abominations. These folks were continuing to observe the Sabbaths, feasts, new moons and special days just as God had commanded, yet *at the same time* were committing horrible atrocities. It was their *hypocrisy*, tainting their sacrifices and feasts, that God so abhorred – not the holy days themselves which He had invented! If new moon observances *themselves* are somehow evil by nature, then – following the same logic in this paragraph – so must be the other things listed here: Sabbaths, appointed feasts, offerings, convocations, incense and prayer! We know these things are not inherently evil, for God is the one who commanded all these things to be done in the first place.

Therefore, let no one act as your judge...

Colossians 2:16

Doesn't Paul warn against new moons?

People who oppose any observance or recognition of Rosh Chodesh will sometimes quote the following scripture from a letter by the apostle Paul (also known as *Rav Sha'ul*, his Hebrew appellation):

> Therefore let no one act as your judge in regard to food or drink or in respect to a festival or a **new moon** or a sabbath day... (Colossians 2:16)

In answer to this, we of course heartily agree with everything it has to say. No one should be acting as anyone's judge in regard to keeping any holy day, whether judging them for **keeping it**, or for **not keeping it**.

This scripture is quoted by people who are concerned that someone might try to require them to observe new moons, festivals and sabbaths, yet the actual context of this letter to the Colossians was the reverse situation! We think that **Paul wrote these words to encourage believers in Colossae to use their freedom** *to observe* **God's holy days in the face of strong cultural opposition.**

The entire context of the chapter describes the challenge facing the believers there. It is highly unlikely that anyone from the pagan culture of Colossae was attempting to force the observance of God's holy days upon these believers. We do know that certain **man-made** commandments and teachings, especially those of the Gnostics, were making an overwhelming, deceitful attack upon the pure faith of the believers there. *Gnostics* believed in salvation through *secret knowledge,* and taught that *matter* (whether the physical universe or the human body) was *inherently evil.* They taught that God could not have created matter, because He was too pure to have anything to do with it. Humans were supposedly "little droplets" of the same good essence that God was made of, but trapped inside physical bodies of evil material. The only way to "salvation" was escape from the body. Some Gnostics, then, treated their bodies very severely. The very idea that Jesus would *choose* to become flesh was sickening to Gnostics.

Paul, recognizing the spiritual and cultural battle swirling around these believers, wrote in this same chapter:

> Be careful that you don't let anyone rob you through his philosophy and vain deceit, **after the tradition of men,** after the elements of the world, and not after Christ (Colossians 2:8, emphasis ours).

> If you died with Christ from the elements of the world, why, as though living in the world, do you subject yourselves to ordinances, "Don't handle, nor taste, nor touch" (all of which perish with use), **according to the precepts and doctrines of men?** Which things indeed appear like wisdom in self-imposed worship, and humility, and **severity to the body**; but aren't of any value against the indulgence of the flesh (Colossians 2:20-23, emphasis ours).

Adding to his argument, Paul actually defends the legitimacy of feasts, sabbaths and new moons in verse 17, citing as evidence of their holiness their crucial role of being a shadow of the Messiah Himself, who is their very "substance" and fulfillment:

> Let no one therefore judge you in eating, or in drinking, or with respect to a feast day or a new moon or a sabbath day, which are a shadow of the things to come; but the body [the substance, the reality] that casts it belongs to Christ. (Colossians 2:16-17)

Speaking of "things to come," another scripture shows that there continues to be an ongoing role for God's new moons and sabbaths. The prophet Isaiah, speaking about some future glorious time, writes, "It shall happen, that **from one new moon to another, and from one sabbath to another,** shall all flesh come to worship before me, says the LORD" (Isaiah 66:23). As a student of the eminent rabbi Gamaliel, Paul was well familiar with this verse and all of its practical implications.

Paul expended much effort countering false teachings. Taking the view that Colossians 2 as a whole is a *warning against Gnosticism* permits verse 16 to be validly interpreted as Paul's *defense of anyone who chooses to follow a Biblical calendar.*

The other interpretation

Some people view Colossians 2:16-17 in the exact opposite sense, and we can certainly see validity in their point of view. They would claim that, since the reality and substance is Messiah, Paul was stating there was no reason for these Gentiles to be judged for *declining* to keep certain feasts, sabbaths and new moons. After all, they say, once we have the actual Messiah living within us, these special days can only pale in comparison, being mere shadows of His great reality.

We agree completely that all God's days and seasons were established by Him *in service of Him*, not in service of some annual calendar. Their whole intent is to point us toward Messiah. In fact, glorification of Jesus is their entire function. Whether that function is best achieved by *non-observance* for some, or by *observance* for others, really depends on the individual. We have witnessed good results in either situation, and we rejoice to witness true salvation and growth in Messiah, no matter how it comes about. (In the spirit of full disclosure, though, we must admit that we ourselves have received *great* blessing and joy in observing God's calendar, drawing closer to Jesus and understanding His Word more deeply. For that reason, our general tendency is to encourage folks to prayerfully investigate God's calendar and be open to however the Holy Spirt might lead.)

No matter which interpretation you believe to be correct, the spirit of this law is clear. It is actually a very simple thing to obey this commandment recorded by Paul. We must never judge or shun one another, whether it be for **observing** God's special days, or for **not observing** God's special days. Let us, in complete freedom – and in complete unity – spend *every* day of our lives in reverent service of our LORD Yeshua.

All of God's days and seasons were established by Him, in service of Him.

An overview of the names of the months

Just like the days of the week, the Biblical months were originally just numbered: the *first* month, the *second* month, etc.

Early in Israel's history, four of the months received actual names. They were:

Abib, the name given to the first month

Ziv, the name given to the second month

Etanim, the name given to the seventh month

Bul, the name given to the eighth month.

These four names, occurring **before** the Babylonian exile, are called the **pre-exilic** names. You might see these names sprinkled throughout the Old Testament, but they are not always used explicitly. Scripture alternately refers to the month of Abib, for example, as either *Abib* or just *the first month*. The modern equivalent would be alternately choosing to write "June 19" (using the month's *name*) or "6/19" (using the month's *number*).

With trumpets and the blast of the ram's horn, shout triumphantly in the presence of the LORD, our King.
– Psalm 98:6

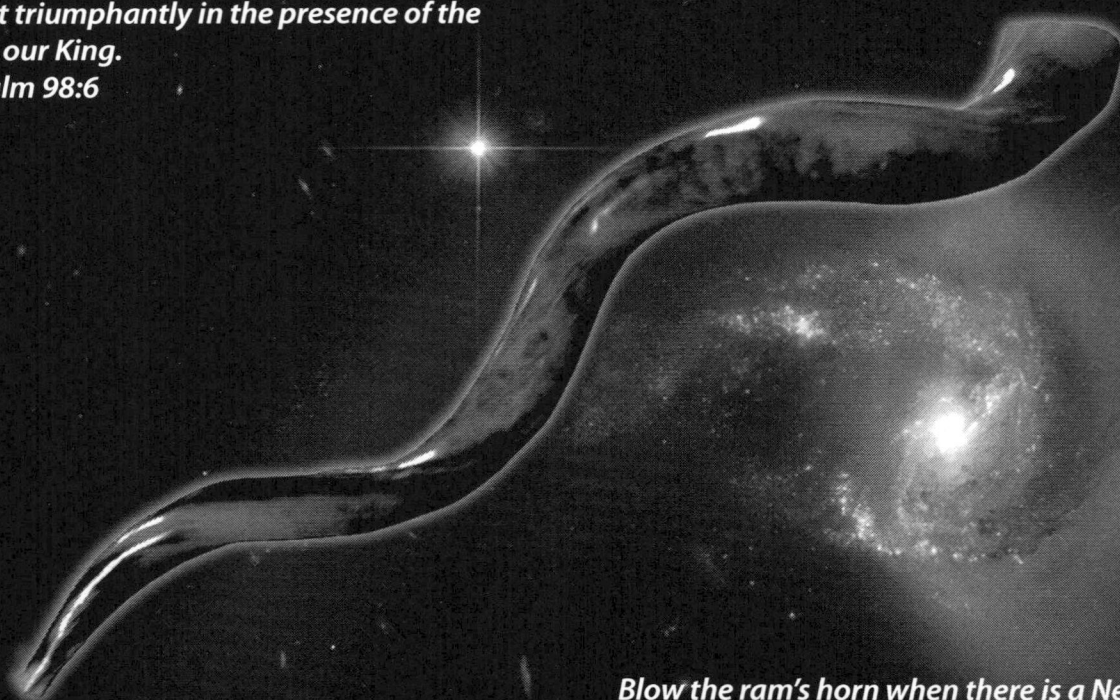

Blow the ram's horn when there is a New Moon...
– Psalm 81:3

After the Babylonian exile, Israel's calendar was indelibly marked. All twelve of the months came to be called by *Babylonian* names. Some believe that God allowed these name changes so that the Jewish people could never forget that awful time of chastening in the land of Babylon – a monthly reminder to stay true to God in the future. These names are the **post-exilic** names of the months, because they came about **after** the exile. Here they are.

> *Nisan*, the name given to the first month
>
> *Iyar*, the name given to the second month
>
> *Sivan*, the name given to the third month
>
> *Tammuz*, the name given to the fourth month
>
> *Av*, the name given to the fifth month
>
> *Elul*, the name given to the sixth month
>
> *Tishri* or *Tishrei*, the name given to the seventh month
>
> *Cheshvan* or *Marcheshvan*, the name given to the eighth month
>
> *Kislev*, the name given to the ninth month
>
> *Tevet*, the name given to the tenth month
>
> *Shevat*, the name given to the eleventh month
>
> *Adar*, the name given to the twelfth month

You will notice that the Biblical lunar calendar has twelve months in the year, like the western calendar. However, since there are slightly more than twelve moon phase cycles in any agricultural or solar year, occasionally there needs to be a thirteenth month added to certain years, a "second Adar," (Adar II or *Adar shay-NEE* in Hebrew). This permits the lunar cycles and the solar cycle to "catch up" with each other when needed (similar to the western calendar "leap year"). On Biblical calendars, you will notice an Adar I *and* an Adar II during these special "leap" years.

In the next section, we will show you how the Biblical months are arranged within the Biblical *year*.

The months of the Bible may be referred to either by number or by name.

The Biblical Year

MONTH 1	MONTH 2	MONTH 3	MONTH 4	MONTH 5	MONTH 6
Post-Exilic Name:	Post-Exilic Name:	Post-Exilic Name:	Post-Exilic Name:	Post-Exilic Name:	Post-Exilic Name:
Nisan	**Iyar**	**Sivan**	**Tammuz**	**Av**	**Elul**
נִיסָן	אִיָּיר	סִיוָן	תָּמוּז	אָב	אֱלוּל
nee–SAHN	*ee–YAR*	*see–VAHN*	*tah–MOOZ*	*ahv*	*eh–LOOL*
Pre-Exilic Name:	Pre-Exilic Name:				
Abib	**Ziv**				
אָבִיב	זִו				
ah–VEEV	*ziv*				
Agriculture in Israel	*Agriculture in Israel*	*Agriculture in Israel*	*Agriculture in Israel*	*Agriculture in Israel*	*Agriculture in Israel*
Spring Equinox	Summer	Wheat harvest	Wheat harvest	Principal fruit	Dates and
Latter rains	Dry season begins	Early figs ripen	Early grape	month:	Summer figs
Barley harvest	Barley harvest		harvest	Grape, fig, olive	
Flax harvest	continues				
Biblical Holy Days		*Biblical Holy Days*			
Pesach (Passover)		Shavuot (Weeks,			
Chag Ha Matzah		or Pentecost)			
(Unleavened Bread)					
Yom Ha Bikkurim					
(Firstfruits)					

—March—→ ←—April—→ ←—May—→ ←—June—→ ←—July—→ ←—August—→ ←—Sept.

This section begins with a graphic showing the order of the Biblical months as they occur throughout the year. The graphic spans both pages. Take a moment to read it over carefully.

On the following pages we will discuss the Biblical year in greater detail.

FALL **WINTER**

MONTH 7	MONTH 8	MONTH 9	MONTH 10	MONTH 11	MONTH 12
Post-Exilic Name:	Post-Exilic Name:	Post-Exilic Name:	Post-Exilic Name:	Post-Exilic Name:	Post-Exilic Name:
Tishrei תִּשְׁרֵי	**Cheshvan** חֶשְׁוָן	**Kislev** כִּסְלֵב	**Tevet** טֵבֵת	**Shevat** שְׁבָט	**Adar** אֲדָר
tish-ray or תִּשְׁרִי *tish-ree*	*chesh-VAHN*	*kiss-layv*	*tay-VAYT*	*sh'-VAHT*	*ah-DAR*
					אֲדָר שֵׁנִי *ah-DAR shay-NEE* (Second Adar), a 13th month, is sometimes added to ensure Nisan16 occurs after the Spring Equinox.
Pre-Exilic Name:	Pre-Exilic Name:				
Etanim אֵתָנִים	**Bul** בּוּל				
ay-tah-NEEM	*bool*				
Agriculture in Israel Early rains Seedtime Plowing & sowing	*Agriculture in Israel* Wheat and Barley sowing	*Agriculture in Israel* Winter begins	*Agriculture in Israel* Rainy winter months Cultivation of Jordan Valley begins	*Agriculture in Israel* Almond blossoms Oranges ripening	*Agriculture in Israel* Barley ripening Citrus fruit harvest
Biblical Holy Days Yom Teruah (Day of Trumpets) Yom Kippur (Day of Atonement) Sukkot (Tabernacles)		*Biblical Event* Chanukah (Festival of the Rededication of the Temple) (John 10:22)			*Biblical Event* Purim (Memorial of God's deliverance of His people in the book of Esther)

Sept. ⟶ ⟵ October ⟶ ⟵ November ⟶ ⟵ December ⟶ ⟵ January ⟶ ⟵ February ⟶ ⟵ March

Top things to know about the Biblical year

As with all things Biblical, there is such a richness and depth of knowledge about the Biblical calendar that you could spend an eternity mining the Word of God and never stop. In this section, we'll try to provide the *essentials* about the Biblical year. You will gradually absorb more information as you study each month in detail, in later sections of this book.

Seven major "appointed times" of the LORD

On the graphic on the preceding pages, we indicated some of the "Biblical Holy Days." These special days, designated by God as holy, are usually referred to in scripture by the Hebrew word מוֹעֲדִים *mo-ah-DEEM*, **appointed times** (from the singular noun מוֹעֵד *mo-AYD*, meaning *appointed time, place or meeting*). These appointed times are sometimes translated "feasts," but not all of them involve feasting (one of them is actually a fast day).

The seven major appointed times are described in detail in Leviticus 23, in which He describes His invention of these days of "holy assembly" and tells the people exactly what day of each month they are to be observed. God begins the chapter with the following key words:

> The LORD spoke to Moses, saying, "Speak to the children of Israel, and tell them, 'The appointed times of the LORD, which you shall proclaim to be holy convocations, even these are My appointed times.'" (Lev. 23:1-2)

Notice the strong sense of personal ownership in verse 2. God calls them "My appointed times." It's important to remember that the people of Israel did not create these observances. The reason this fact is so important to keep in mind is because of the *prophetic significance* of God's appointed times.

The prophetic significance of the seven major appointed times

It's outside the scope of this book to discuss the full prophetic meaning of the **Lord's appointed times**, or **moadim** *(mo-ah-DEEM)*, for there is too much wonderful information to share in this limited space. There are many, many other books which address this glorious topic in great detail (and we strongly suggest you read one of them upon completion of this book). Here, we will provide very brief descriptions so that you may have at least a basic understanding of their significance as you learn about their place in God's Biblical year. The *moadim* have been set by God to occur in two time periods: **spring and fall.** These two time periods correspond to the first and second comings of Jesus the Messiah. Very briefly, here are the ultimate prophetic fulfillments of the *moadim*:

The SPRING *moadim* – fulfillment completed

Passover *(Pesach)* – Nisan 14, the date of Yeshua's crucifixion

Feast of Unleavened Bread *(Chag Ha Matzah)* – Nisan 15-21, a seven-day feast during which Yeshua was in the tomb

Feast of Firstfruits *(Yom Ha Bikkurim)* – Nisan 16, the date of Yeshua's resurrection

Feast of Weeks/Pentecost *(Shavuot)* – Sivan 6, the date that the believers in Acts chapter 2 were filled with the indwelling Holy Spirit

The FALL *moadim* – fulfillment in the future

Day of Trumpets *(Yom Teruah)* – Tishri 1, signifying the future translation of believers (aka *the Rapture*)

Day of Atonement *(Yom Kippur)* – Tishri 10, signifying the future atonement of all of the believing remnant of Israel

Tabernacles *(Sukkot)* – Tishri 15-21, a seven-day feast with an additional eighth day of assembly on Tishri 22, signifying the future millennial (thousand-year) reign of Yeshua on earth

There isn't enough space in one book to describe the glory of God's appointed times.

Who decided the timing of the months and the beginning of the Biblical year?

Two great questions we are often asked by students are, "Does anyone know how it was decided that the month *Nisan* should occur in *spring*?" and "Who decided that the *beginning* of the year, the *first* month, had to be the month *Nisan*?" These two questions are both answered by the following scripture:

> The LORD spoke to Moses and Aaron in the land of Egypt, saying, "This month shall be to you the beginning of months. It shall be the first month of the year to you" (Ex. 12:1-2).

So, **the LORD decided which month would be the start of the Biblical year, and in which season He wanted it to occur.** What is the context of this verse? The people of Israel are still enslaved in Egypt, and Pharoah has hardened his heart so many times that God is ready to bring the angel of death upon Egypt to kill their firstborn children. Here, in Exodus 12, God gives instructions for the slaughtering of the passover lamb, so that the angel of death would pass over the houses of the children of Israel. This is the very first passover in human history. In verse 14 of this chapter, God says that this day, the Passover, shall be celebrated as a memorial, as a "permanent ordinance throughout your generations." In the next chapter, God says, "This day you go forth in the month Abib" (Exodus 13:4). Later, we read in Deuteronomy 16:1, "Observe the month of Abib and celebrate the Passover to the LORD your God, for in the month of Abib the LORD your God brought you out of Egypt by night."

Therefore, we know that God Himself chose the month *Abib* – later known as *Nisan* – to be the *first* month of the Biblical year.

According to God's plan, the Jewish people were allowed *zero input* into the design of the Biblical calendar, including the most basic decision about which month should be the first one in the year. **The Biblical calendar, then, is technically not a *Jewish* calendar, for it was not invented by human beings.** The reason God's calendar ever came to be called the "Jewish calendar" is because the first people to receive it were Jewish, and they were the predominant group who consistently observed it (later joined by born-again Gentiles, many of whom observed it during the first three centuries following Yeshua's resurrection). **God's calendar, like the Bible itself, was intended to be shared with the entire world, like a light to the nations – not restricted to only one ethnic group.**

The Biblical calendar is a *free gift* that God has made available to *anyone* who loves Him. Are you feeling drawn to participate? You're allowed (yes, even if you're not Jewish) to join the fun! When it comes to God's festivals, we're *all* invited!

The Biblical years are grouped in "sevens"

Now that we have learned about the arrangement of the months and appointed times within the Biblical year, let's turn our attention to *groups of years*.

We all know how much God loves the number *seven*, for He ordained it as *the number of completion*. He designed the week to be seven days long, then rested on the seventh day. This pattern of sevens appears throughout scripture in many contexts, and we see the term *week* (generally meaning *a group of seven*) applied to other things besides days. Think of the old-fashioned meaning for "week" more like the way we use the word "dozen." Just as a *dozen* means *twelve of something*, a *week* means *seven of something*. For example, "a week of years" just means "seven years".

Sabbath years – when the *land* rests

Scripture teaches that God established such a thing as a *sabbath year*.

> The LORD said to Moses in Mount Sinai, "Speak to the children of Israel, and tell them, 'When you come into the land which I give you, then the **land shall keep a Sabbath** to the LORD. Six years you shall sow your field, and six years you shall prune your vineyard, and gather in its fruits; but in the seventh year there shall be **a Sabbath of solemn rest for the land, a Sabbath to the LORD.** You shall not sow your field or prune your vineyard'" (Lev. 25:1-4).

In the scripture above, the word *Sabbath* is the same exact Hebrew word as the one used for the weekly Sabbath – *shabbat*, שַׁבָּת.

After *seven* such sabbath years had passed – that is, seven times seven years or 49 total years – there is a very special sabbath year on the *fiftieth* year called a **jubilee year.** It, too, is a year of rest for the land, but also a year that everyone is liberated in order to return to his own property. You can read the complete details about the year of jubilee in Leviticus 25:8-54. The word *jubilee* comes from the Hebrew in the text, *yo-VAYL*, יוֹבֵל, meaning *a ram's horn used as a wind instrument*. The reason God named the jubilee year after this ram's horn instrument is explained by His words in Leviticus 25:8-10.

> You shall count off **seven Sabbaths of years**, seven times seven years; and there shall be to you the days of seven Sabbaths of years, even **forty-nine years.** Then you shall **sound the loud trumpet**... You shall make the **fiftieth year holy**, and proclaim liberty throughout the land to all its inhabitants. It shall be a **jubilee** to you; and each of you shall return to his own property, and each of you shall return to his family.

This completes our overview of God's Biblical *day, week, month* and *year*, which provides a firm foundation for the remainder of this book. The next page begins the sections which feature each month individually.

> *"...in the seventh year there shall be a Sabbath of solemn rest for the land, a Sabbath to the LORD..."*
>
> Leviticus 25:4, the words of God

Purge out the old leaven,
that you may be a new lump,
even as you are unleavened.
For indeed Messiah,
our Passover, has been
sacrificed in our place.

1 Corinthians 5:7

The First Month

This section begins the portion of our book in which we learn about each month in detail, each in its own section. In this particular section, we will study about the month **Nisan** *(nee-SAHN)*, also known by its earlier, pre-exilic name, **Abib** *(ah-BEEB)*. This month corresponds to the western months of March/April.

Important Biblical appointed times or events in this month include:

- **Passover** – the redemption from Egypt and its symbolism of Messiah's sacrificial death (Lev. 23:5, 1 Cor. 5:7)

- **Unleavened Bread** – its symbolism of a life free from sin, as well as Messiah's burial (Lev. 23:6-8, 1 Cor. 5:7, 2 Cor. 5:21)

- **Firstfruits** – and its fulfillment in Messiah's resurrection (Lev. 23:15, 1 Cor. 15:20-23)

- **Counting of the *Omer* (Sheaf)** – the fifty-day countdown to Pentecost (Weeks) begins (Lev. 23:15-16)

Another very important Biblical event was **the setting up of the tabernacle** on the first day of Nisan, by God's command. God's chosen date of Nisan 1 for the inauguration of His first-ever communal worship location vividly demonstrates His *personal ownership* of the Biblical calendar year. God's cloud of glory so filled this tabernacle that not even Moses could enter (Ex. 40:2, 17, 34-35).

About this section

On the next two pages, we have provided a **date graphic** displaying the days of the month of Nisan. Each day is represented by a photograph of the moon as it appears on that date. This graphic displays significant events which either occurred *once* on a particular date (historic, one-time events), or *repeating* events that occur every year (annual holy days, for example). Note that the graphic is not intended to portray the events in chronological order of their occurrence in history by *year*. It only portrays the *date* on which each event occurred – much like the list of employee birthdays at the office shows all their *dates* of birth in order, but disregards their *years* of birth.

Following the graphic, we provided a **list of all the scriptures** in both the Old and New Testaments (where applicable), which contain the Hebrew (or Greek) terms for *first month*, *Nisan*, or *Abib*. Take time to carefully study the graphic and then read all the scripture references. You will be greatly blessed by it!

> *"This month shall be to you the beginning of months. It shall be the first month of the year to you."*
>
> *Exodus 12:2, the words of God*

Nisan / Abib

Each date of the month is shown inside the moon images. For example, Nisan 1, the first day of Nisan, is indicated by the numeral 1 in the graphic below. *Biblical* events are shown *above* the graphic. *Historical* events which are not mentioned in scripture are shown *below* the graphic.*** Due to limited space on the graphic, only key, selected events are included (there are more Biblical and historical events which occurred in this month than we can display). **Please note that the events on this graphic are *not* shown in the order in which they actually occurred in history... just the *date* on which they occurred.** The graphic does not really work like a history timeline; it is more like an office birthday list showing each employee's *month* and *day* of birth, while disregarding the *years* they were born.)

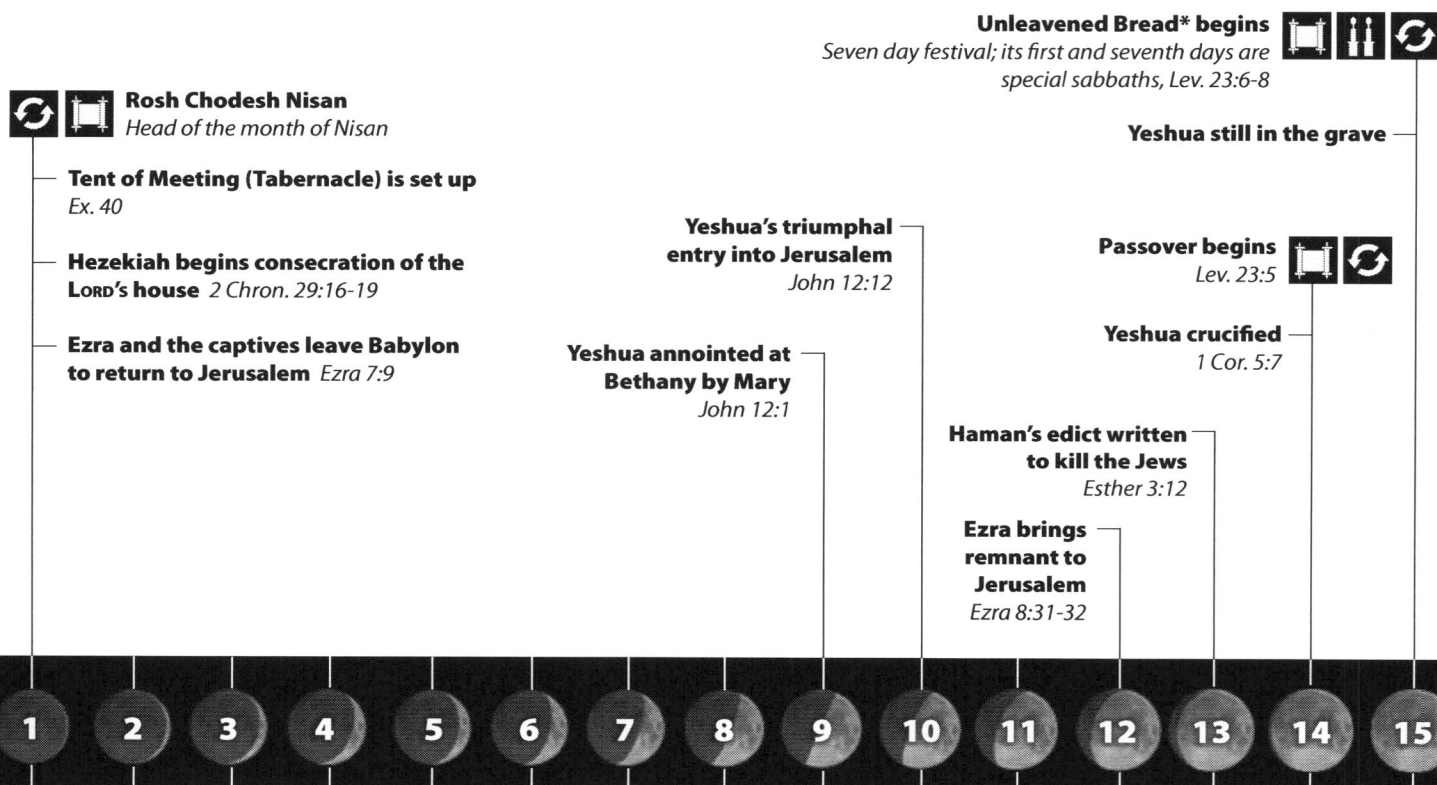

Unleavened Bread* begins
Seven day festival; its first and seventh days are
special sabbaths, Lev. 23:6-8

Rosh Chodesh Nisan
Head of the month of Nisan

Yeshua still in the grave

Tent of Meeting (Tabernacle) is set up
Ex. 40

Yeshua's triumphal entry into Jerusalem
John 12:12

Passover begins
Lev. 23:5

Hezekiah begins consecration of the LORD's house 2 Chron. 29:16-19

Yeshua crucified
1 Cor. 5:7

Ezra and the captives leave Babylon to return to Jerusalem Ezra 7:9

Yeshua annointed at Bethany by Mary
John 12:1

Haman's edict written to kill the Jews
Esther 3:12

Ezra brings remnant to Jerusalem
Ezra 8:31-32

| 1 | 2 | 3 | 4 | 5 | 6 | 7 | 8 | 9 | 10 | 11 | 12 | 13 | 14 | 15 |

Warsaw Ghetto uprising begins
1943 CE

Aliyah Day
Yom Ha Aliyah, Immigration Day, an Israeli national holiday. "Aliyah" is Hebrew for "ascent, going up," signifying the physically elevated position of Jerusalem as well as the spiritually elevated position of that city and all of God's holy land. Religious Jews (and many Gentiles) view entry into Israel and Jerusalem as an opportunity for repentance – a personal spiritual "ascent." This day coincides with Jesus' triumphal entry into Jerusalem.

Passover/Unleavened Bread Nisan 15-21, Israeli national holiday (days off for schools, government offices and many businesses in Israel)

Key:

[icon] "Appointed time" or other observance established by God in scripture

[icon] Special Annual Sabbath (not necessarily falling on the seventh day of a week)

[icon] Commemorated event in Israel's history or Israeli national holiday

[icon] Event commanded by God to be observed annually

*New Testament writers often used the terms "Unleavened Bread" and "Passover" interchangeably, because in daily conversation, people loosely referred to the general time period between Nisan 14 and 21 by either term. The LORD Himself refers to them as a unit block of time in Ezekiel 45:21.

**In Bible times (as today), if an activity occurred during a small "portion" of a day, it still was said to have occurred "on" that day. The span of time that Jesus was actually in the grave began in the latest hours of Nisan 14, continued through all the hours of Nisan 15, and extended into the earliest hours of Nisan 16 – thus, spanning three separate Biblical days. Here is an excellent example of why it is crucial to understand that the Biblical day begins at sundown; it provides an accurate reconciling of the New Testament accounts of Jesus' time spent in the grave.

Firstfruits
Held the "day after the sabbath," i.e. the day after the special sabbath of Nisan 15, Lev. 23:15

Yeshua resurrected**
1 Cor. 15:20

Counting of the Omer (the sheaf) begins
Fifty-day countdown culminating in the day of Pentecost (Feast of Weeks, Shavuot), Lev. 23:15-16

Last Day of Unleavened Bread
A special sabbath God commanded to mark the end of the seven-day festival, Lev. 23:6-8

Daniel's vision by the Tigris River
Dan. 10:4-9

16 17 18 19 20 21 22 23 24 25 26 27 28 29 30

Yom HaShoah
Holocaust Remembrance Day

Scriptures using the terms *the first month, Nisan or Abib*

The following scriptures mention the *first month* of the Biblical year, either by name or by number order. The list below is not in strict chronological historical order. Instead, this list follows the order of the books of the Bible. We decided on this order because we wanted to make it easier to look up the references one after another, should you desire to read them in their full context in your own Bible. We strongly encourage you to do so. In our classes, we have discovered that students benefit most by turning to each passage in their own Bibles, underlining or circling each mention of the phrase "first month" in their Bible, then jotting the names *Nisan/Abib* next to it in the margins.

In all our scripture lists, we show the Hebrew or Greek terms for each stated month just as they appear in the original texts.

Exodus 12:1-2 *God establishes the first month of the year*

The LORD spoke to Moses and Aaron in the land of Egypt, saying, "This month shall be to you the beginning of months. It shall be the **first month** רִאשׁוֹן of the year to you."

Exodus 12:18 *God's commandment to eat unleavened bread (context verses 17–20)*

"**In the first month** בָּרִאשֹׁן , on the fourteenth day of the month at evening, you shall eat unleavened bread, until the twenty-first day of the month at evening."

Exodus 13:4 *Moses speaks to Israel about leaving Egypt (context verses 1–5)*

"This day you go forth **in the month Abib** בְּחֹדֶשׁ הָאָבִיב ."

Exodus 23:14-15 *God commands Israel to keep the Feast of Unleavened Bread*

"You shall observe a feast to Me three times a year. You shall observe the feast of unleavened bread. Seven days you shall eat unleavened bread, as I commanded you, at the time appointed in **the month Abib** חֹדֶשׁ הָאָבִיב , for in it you came out from Egypt..."

Exodus 34:18 *God repeats His commandment regarding the Feast of Unleavened Bread*

"You shall keep the feast of unleavened bread. Seven days you shall eat unleavened bread, as I commanded you, at the time appointed in **the month Abib** חֹדֶשׁ הָאָבִיב ; for **in the month Abib** בְּחֹדֶשׁ הָאָבִיב you came out from Egypt."

Exodus 40:2 *God instructs Moses regarding the tabernacle (context verses 1–11)*

"On the first day of **the first month** הַחֹדֶשׁ הָרִאשׁוֹן you shall raise up the tabernacle of the Tent of Meeting."

Exodus 40:17 *Moses sets up the tabernacle (context verses 17–19)*

It happened **in the first month** בַּחֹדֶשׁ הָרִאשׁוֹן in the second year, on the first day of the month, that the tabernacle was raised up.

Leviticus 23:5 *God speaks regarding His holy day of passover (context verses 4–5)*

"**In the first month** בַּחֹדֶשׁ הָרִאשׁוֹן , on the fourteenth day of the month in the evening, is the LORD's Passover."

Numbers 9:1 *God commands the celebration of His feast of Passover (context verses 1–5)*

The LORD spoke to Moses in the wilderness of Sinai, **in the first month** בַּחֹדֶשׁ הָרִאשׁוֹן of the second year after they had come out of the land of Egypt...

Numbers 20:1 *Israel reaches Kadesh, Miriam dies*

The children of Israel, even the whole congregation, came into the wilderness of Zin **in the first month** בַּחֹדֶשׁ הָרִאשׁוֹן : and the people stayed in Kadesh; and Miriam died there, and was buried there.

Numbers 28:16 *God speaks these words to Moses to tell the sons of Israel*

"And in the **first month** וּבַחֹדֶשׁ הָרִאשׁוֹן , on the fourteenth day of the month, is the LORD's Passover."

Numbers 33:3 *Retelling of the exodus (context verses 1–4)*

They traveled from Rameses **in the first month** בַּחֹדֶשׁ הָרִאשׁוֹן , on the fifteenth day **of the first month** לַחֹדֶשׁ הָרִאשׁוֹן ; on the next day after the Passover the children of Israel went out with a high hand in the sight of all the Egyptians.

Deuteronomy 16:1 *Moses repeats God's command to observe Abib and Passover (context verses 1–8)*

"Observe **the month of Abib** חֹדֶשׁ הָאָבִיב , and keep the Passover to the LORD your God; for **in the month of Abib** בְּחֹדֶשׁ הָאָבִיב the LORD your God brought you forth out of Egypt by night."

Joshua 4:19 *Israel reaches Jericho after crossing the Jordan River (context verses 15–24)*

The people came up out of the Jordan on the tenth day of **the first month** הָרִאשׁוֹן , and encamped in Gilgal, on the east border of Jericho.

1 Chronicles 12:15 *Listing of those who crossed the Jordan*

These are those who went over the Jordan **in the first month** בַּחֹדֶשׁ הָרִאשׁוֹן , when it had overflowed all its banks; and they put to flight all them of the valleys, both toward the east, and toward the west.

1 Chronicles 27:2-3 *David's civil leader – monthly duty schedule (context verses 1–3)*

Over the first division **for the first month** לַחֹדֶשׁ הָרִאשׁוֹן was Jashobeam the son of Zabdiel: and in his division were twenty-four thousand. He was of the children of Perez, the chief of all the captains of the army **for the first month** לַחֹדֶשׁ הָרִאשׁוֹן.

2 Chronicles 29:3 *Hezekiah opens and repairs the doors of the LORD's house (context verses 1–3)*

He, in the first year of his reign, **in the first month** בַּחֹדֶשׁ הָרִאשׁוֹן , opened the doors of the house of the LORD, and repaired them.

2 Chronicles 29:17 *Consecration of the LORD's house (context verses 16–19)*

Now they began on the first day **of the first month** לַחֹדֶשׁ הָרִאשׁוֹן to sanctify, and on the eighth day of the month they came to the porch of the LORD; and they sanctified the house of the LORD in eight days: and on the sixteenth day **of the first month** לַחֹדֶשׁ הָרִאשׁוֹן they finished.

2 Chronicles 35:1 *King Josiah restores the Passover after destroying all the idols in Israel*

Josiah kept a Passover to the LORD in Jerusalem: and they killed the Passover on the fourteenth day **of the first month** לַחֹדֶשׁ הָרִאשׁוֹן .

Ezra 6:19 *The exiles observe Passover after returning to Jerusalem and rebuilding the LORD's house*

The children of the captivity kept the Passover on the fourteenth day **of the first month** לַחֹדֶשׁ הָרִאשׁוֹן .

Ezra 7:9 *Ezra and the captives leave Babylon on Nisan 1 (context verses 6–10)*

For on the first day **of the first month** לַחֹדֶשׁ הָרִאשׁוֹן he began to go up from Babylon; and on the first day of the fifth month he came to Jerusalem, according to the good hand of his God upon him.

Ezra 8:31 *Ezra brings the remnant to Jerusalem (context verses 31–32)*

Then we departed from the river Ahava on the twelfth day **of the first month** לַחֹדֶשׁ הָרִאשׁוֹן , to go to Jerusalem: and the hand of our God was on us, and he delivered us from the hand of the enemy and the bandit by the way.

Ezra 10:17 *Ezra completes investigations of foreign intermarriages*

They finished dealing with all the men who had married foreign women by the first day **of the first month** לַחֹדֶשׁ הָרִאשׁוֹן .

Nehemiah 2:1 *Nehemiah is sad in the king's presence (context verses 1–2)*

It happened **in the month Nisan** בְּחֹדֶשׁ נִיסָן , in the twentieth year of Artaxerxes the king, when wine was before him, that I took up the wine, and gave it to the king. Now I had not been sad in his presence before.

Esther 3:7 *Pur (the lot) is cast before Haman to ascertain the date to kill the Jews*

In the first month בַּחֹדֶשׁ הָרִאשׁוֹן , which is **the month Nisan** חֹדֶשׁ נִיסָן , in the twelfth year of King Ahasuerus, they cast Pur, that is, the lot, before Haman from day to day, and from month to month, and chose the twelfth month, which is the month Adar.

Esther 3:12 *Haman's edict to kill the Jews is written on the thirteenth day of the first month*

Then the king's scribes were called in **on the first month** בַּחֹדֶשׁ הָרִאשׁוֹן , on the thirteenth day of the month; and all that Haman commanded was written to the king's satraps, and to the governors who were over every province, and to the princes of every people, to every province according its writing, and to every people in their language. It was written in the name of King Ahasuerus, and it was sealed with the king's ring.

Ezekiel 29:17 *The Word of the LORD comes to Ezekiel (context verses 17–21)*

It came to pass in the twenty-seventh year, **in the first month** בָּרִאשׁוֹן , in the first day of the month, the word of the LORD came to me, saying...

Ezekiel 30:20 *The Word of the LORD comes to Ezekiel (context verses 20–22)*

It happened in the eleventh year, **in the first month בָּרִאשׁוֹן** , in the seventh day of the month, that the word of the LORD came to me, saying...

Ezekiel 45:18 *The Lord commands the people to cleanse the sanctuary (context verses 18–20)*

"Thus says Adonai the LORD: **In the first month בָּרִאשׁוֹן** , in the first day of the month, you shall take a young bull without blemish; and you shall cleanse the sanctuary."

Ezekiel 45:21 *The Lord commands the people to keep Passover / Unleavened Bread*

"**In the first month בָּרִאשׁוֹן** , in the fourteenth day of the month, you shall have the Passover, a feast of seven days; unleavened bread shall be eaten."

Daniel 10:4 *Daniel's vision by the Tigris River (context verses 4–9)*

In the twenty-fourth day **of the first month לַחֹדֶשׁ הָרִאשׁוֹן** , as I was by the side of the great river, which is Hiddekel...

Joel 2:23 *Joel tells the people to rejoice because of the latter rains being given*

Be glad then, you children of Zion, and rejoice in the LORD, your God; for He gives you the former rain in just measure, and He causes the rain to come down for you, the former rain, and the latter rain **in the first month בָּרִאשׁוֹן** . (Some translations translate this: *latter rain as at the first, latter rain as before,* or *latter rain in the beginning,* rather than *the first month.*)

48 47 46 45

49

50

44

43

42

*Photo showing possible
location of Mt. Horeb / Sinai,
the site of the giving of the
Torah (God's "instruction")*

41

40

33

32

34

31

35

39

38

37

36

"Moses Strikes the
Rock," painting by James
Jacques Joseph Tissot,
c. 1896

30

29

28

24

25

23

27

26

22

"Victory O Lord!" (Battle with
the Amalekites) painting by John
Everett Millais, 1871

21

18

19

20

17

14

16

15

13

12

11

10

9

8

7

6

5

"Gathering of the
Manna," painting by
James Jacques Joseph
Tissot, c. 1896

4

3

2

1

The Second Month

The second month of the Biblical year is also known by its pre-exilic name, **Ziv**, and its post-exilic name, **Iyar** (pronounced *ih-YAR*). It corresponds to April/May in the western calendar.

Biblical themes of the month Iyar

The month of **Iyar** is a "connector month" between **Nisan, the month of deliverance**, and **Sivan, the month of revelation.** *Nisan*, which contains Passover (Yeshua's death), Unleavened Bread (Yeshua's burial) and Firstfruits (Yeshua's resurrection), speaks of God **delivering** Israel from the bondage of Egypt and all mankind from the bondage of sin and death. *Sivan*, which we will study in the section after this one, contains the Feast of Weeks (Shavuot), which is the date of the **revelation** of Torah on Mount Sinai as well as the indwelling Holy Spirit in the book of Acts (on Shavuot, the day of Pentecost).

Iyar, then, is a month of journey and anticipation, suspended between deliverance and revelation. Here are some of its major scriptural themes:

- **Journeying and Preservation** – As the people of Israel journeyed out of Egypt and through the wilderness of Sinai, they were miraculously provided bread from heaven (manna) and water from the rock.

- **Anticipation of Revelation** – God's fifty-day countdown from Firstfruits to Weeks (or Pentecost, meaning "fifty") occurs throughout Iyar (Lev. 23:15-16). God used Israel's first fifty-day journey to learn to depend on Him – to build their faith – in order to be able to receive His Torah. And, after His resurrection, Jesus told His followers to "wait" in Jerusalem for the coming empowering of the Holy Spirit (Acts 1:4). They waited during the month of *Iyar*.

- **Preservation of the Nation** – the first attack on the nation of Israel after they left Egypt was by the Amalekites, in the month Iyar. Moses held up God's staff throughout the battle (Aaron and Hur helped hold his arms up), and the Israelites prevailed. God then stated He would "completely blot out the name of Amalek from under heaven." *Amalek* is the ultimate Biblical archetype of *the enemy of Israel;* Hitler is one of several historical examples of this Amalek archetype.

Historical themes of the month Iyar

In the historical section below the graphic on the next pages are listed many attacks upon the Jews which occurred during Iyar, yet God's people survived. A historical theme of this month might be the *preservation of Israel as a nation.*

> *Then the LORD said to Moses, "I will rain down bread from heaven for you..."*
>
> *Exodus 16:4, the words of God, spoken on the fifteenth day of the month Iyar*

Iyar / Ziv

Throughout the month of Iyar, God's fifty-day countdown from the Feast of Firstfruits to the Feast of Weeks continues. The first attack on the nation of Israel after they left Egypt occurred in Iyar. God miraculously helped Israel defend themselves against the Amalekites and Israel was preserved. Amalek is an archetype of the "enemies of Israel."

Rosh Chodesh Iyar
Head of the month of Iyar

The LORD commands a census of Israel be taken *Num. 1:1-3*

Solomon begins construction of the temple
2 Chron. 3:1-2

Israel murmurs against the LORD in the wilderness of Sin; God provides manna in response
Ex. 16:1-4

God makes a provision for an "alternate" Passover
Num. 9:10-12

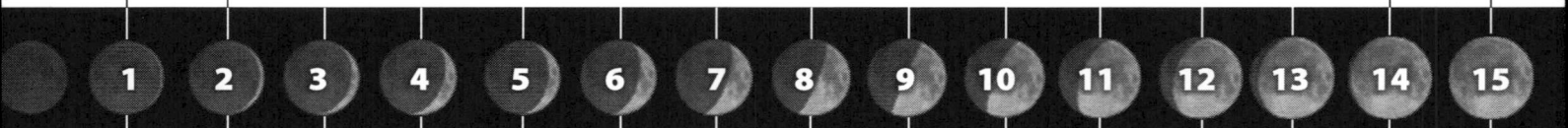

| 1 | 2 | 3 | 4 | 5 | 6 | 7 | 8 | 9 | 10 | 11 | 12 | 13 | 14 | 15 |

Yom Ha Atzma'ut
Israel's "Day of Independence" commemorating the Israeli Declaration of Independence in 1948

First Crusade Pogroms Begin
1096

Herzl Day
Israeli national holiday celebrating the life of Zionist Theodor Herzl

Jews expelled from Bern, Switzerland
1427

Books confiscated – *1500 Jewish books confiscated in Frankfurt am Main, Germany, 1510*

Three years of Pogroms in Russia *begin, 1881*

Battle at Degania – *Israeli Army defeats the advancing Syrian Army in 1948. Considered the first Israeli victory of the War of Independence.*

Jews of Bisenz, Austria massacred, *1605*

Books burned – *Nazis burn thousands of books written by Jews, 1933*

Adolf Eichmann captured in Buenos Aires, *1960*

Jews expelled from Ukraine, *1727*

Rostov-on-Don Pogrom, *1883*

Nuremburg Laws – *Nazi laws depriving Jews of citizenship rights passed in 1935*

Dachau liberated, *1945*

Key:

"Appointed time" or other observance established by God in scripture

Special Annual Sabbath (not necessarily falling on the seventh day of a week)

Commemorated event in Israel's history or Israeli national holiday

Event commanded by God to be observed annually

Israel leaves Sinai for Paran
Num. 10:11-12

16 17 18 19 20 21 22 23 24 25 26 27 28 29

Yom Yerushalayim
"Jerusalem Day"
Reunification of Jerusalem, 1967

Six-Day War begins, *1967*

Toledo Massacre, *1200 Jews massacred, 1355*

Cologne Jews saved *during first Crusade, 1096*

Germany surrenders to Allied Forces, *1945*

Nazis deport Hungarian Jews to Auschwitz, *100,000 killed in eight days, 1944*

Jewish books begin to be confiscated *by the Vatican in all Papal provinces over a 20 year period, 1731*

All pregnant women of Kovno ghetto sentenced to death *by the Nazis, 1942*

Venice Jews forbidden to practice law, *1637*

Goebbels commits suicide, *1945*

Lag Ba'Omer *33rd Day of the Omer Count, memorializing the end of a plague which killed 24,000 of Rabbi Akiva's disciples, as well as the death of Rabbi Shimon bar Yochai. This day is commonly held as a day of celebration. Weddings are often held on this day.*

Ettingen Jews acquitted of blood libel *and their synagogue spared, 1690*

IDF (Israeli Defense Forces) *created, 1948*

Hurva Synagogue dynamited *during battle for Old Jerusalem, 1948. "The Hurva" means "The Ruin;" the synagogue had been destroyed earlier in 1721 and rebuilt.*

Roman garrison defeated *in Jerusalem by the Jews, after the theft of silver from the Temple, 66 CE*

Scriptures using the terms *the second month, Iyar or Ziv*

Exodus 16:1 *Israel murmurs against God, God provides manna (context verses 1–4)*

They took their journey from Elim, and all the congregation of the children of Israel came to the wilderness of Sin, which is between Elim and Sinai, on the fifteenth day **of the second month** לַחֹדֶשׁ הַשֵּׁנִי after their departing out of the land of Egypt.

Numbers 1:1-2 *God commands Moses to take a census of the sons of Israel (context verses 1–4)*

The LORD spoke to Moses in the wilderness of Sinai, in the Tent of Meeting, on the first day **of the second month** לַחֹדֶשׁ הַשֵּׁנִי, in the second year after they had come out of the land of Egypt, saying, "Take a census of all the congregation of the children of Israel, by their families, by their fathers' houses, according to the number of the names, every male, one by one..."

Numbers 1:18 *Godly census of Israel is taken (context verses 17–19)*

They assembled all the congregation together on the first day **of the second month** לַחֹדֶשׁ הַשֵּׁנִי; and they declared their ancestry by their families, by their fathers' houses, according to the number of the names, from twenty years old and upward, one by one.

Numbers 9:10-11 *God's provision of an alternate Passover (context verses 10–12)*

"Say to the children of Israel, 'If any man of you or of your generations is unclean by reason of a dead body, or is on a journey far away, he shall still keep the Passover to the LORD. **In the second month** בַּחֹדֶשׁ הַשֵּׁנִי, on the fourteenth day at evening they shall keep it; they shall eat it with unleavened bread and bitter herbs.'"

Numbers 10:11-12 *Israel leaves Sinai for Paran*

It happened in the second year, **in the second month** בַּחֹדֶשׁ הַשֵּׁנִי, on the twentieth day of the month, that the cloud was taken up from over the tabernacle of the testimony. The children of Israel went forward according to their journeys out of the wilderness of Sinai; and the cloud stayed in the wilderness of Paran.

1 Kings 6:1 *Solomon begins construction of the temple*

It happened in the four hundred and eightieth year after the children of Israel were come out of the land of Egypt, in the fourth year of Solomon's reign over Israel, **in the month Ziv** בְּחֹדֶשׁ זִו, which is **the second month** הַחֹדֶשׁ הַשֵּׁנִי, that he began to build the house of the LORD.

1 Kings 6:37 *Solomon lays the foundation for the temple*

In the fourth year was the foundation of the house of the LORD laid, in the month **Ziv** זִו .

1 Chronicles 27:4 *David's civil leader — monthly duty schedule*

Over the division of **the second month** הַחֹדֶשׁ הַשֵּׁנִי was Dodai the Ahohite, and his division; and Mikloth the ruler: and in his division were twenty-four thousand.

2 Chronicles 3:1-2 *Solomon begins construction of the temple*

Then Solomon began to build the house of the LORD at Jerusalem on Mount Moriah, where the LORD appeared to David his father, which he prepared in the place that David had appointed, in the threshing floor of Ornan the Jebusite. He began to build in the second day **of the second month** בַּחֹדֶשׁ הַשֵּׁנִי , in the fourth year of his reign.

2 Chronicles 30:2-3 *Hezekiah invites Israel and Judah to alternate Passover (context verses 1-5)*

For the king had taken counsel, and his princes, and all the assembly in Jerusalem, to keep the Passover **in the second month** בַּחֹדֶשׁ הַשֵּׁנִי . For they had not been able to keep it at that time, because the priests had not sanctified themselves in sufficient number, nor had the people gathered themselves together to Jerusalem.

2 Chronicles 30:13 *Alternate Unleavened Bread celebrated*

Many people assembled at Jerusalem to keep the Feast of Unleavened Bread **in the second month** בַּחֹדֶשׁ הַשֵּׁנִי , a very great assembly.

2 Chronicles 30:15 *Passover lambs killed for alternate Passover*

Then they killed the Passover on the fourteenth day **of the second month** לַחֹדֶשׁ הַשֵּׁנִי : and the priests and the Levites were ashamed, and sanctified themselves, and brought burnt offerings into the house of the LORD.

Ezra 3:8 *Zerubbabel, Jeshua and the people who returned from captivity begin to rebuild the temple*

Now in the second year of their coming to the house of God at Jerusalem, **in the second month** בַּחֹדֶשׁ הַשֵּׁנִי , began Zerubbabel the son of Shealtiel, and Jeshua the son of Jozadak, and the rest of their brothers the priests and the Levites, and all those who were come out of the captivity to Jerusalem, and appointed the Levites, from twenty years old and upward, to have the oversight of the work of the house of the LORD.

...there were thunders and lightnings, and a thick cloud on the mountain, and the sound of an exceedingly loud trumpet...
*All Mount Sinai smoked, because the L*ORD *descended on it in fire; and its smoke ascended like the smoke of a furnace, and the whole mountain quaked greatly...*

Exodus 19:16,18

Now when the day of Pentecost had fully come, they were all with one accord in one place. Suddenly there came from the sky a sound like the rushing of a mighty wind, and it filled all the house where they were sitting. Tongues like fire appeared and were distributed to them, and one sat on each of them.

Acts 2:1-3

The Third Month

The third month of the Biblical year is also known by its post-exilic name, **Sivan** (pronounced *see-VAHN*). It corresponds to May/June in the western calendar.

Biblical themes of the month Sivan

The month **Sivan** contains the **Feast of Weeks** (Hebrew *Shavuot*, meaning *weeks*, or *Pentecost*, from the Greek word for *fifty*). God commanded that, annually, there should be counted a "week of weeks" (i.e., seven weeks or 49 days) starting from the Feast of Firstfruits. God said the fiftieth day should be called "the Feast of Weeks" and made it **a special sabbath** as well as a "pilgrim feast" – a feast to be held in **Jerusalem** (Lev. 23:15-16, Num. 28:26, Deut. 16:9-11).

On Shavuot – Sivan 6 – two pivotal events occurred. Moses and the people received the *Torah* (Hebrew "instruction") at Mount Sinai, AND, centuries later, the believers received the indwelling Holy Spirit at Mount Zion (Jerusalem) as described in Acts 2.

The theme of the month Sivan is God's personal revelation to His people and the sanctification and salvation which results from knowing Him and His ways.

- **The Giving of Torah** – to Moses and the people of Israel at Mount Sinai, Exodus 19

- **The Giving of the Indwelling Holy Spirit** – to the believers at Mount Zion (Jerusalem), Acts 2.

The reason the believers of the book of Acts were in Jerusalem all together in one place on the date of Sivan 6 was two-fold. Yeshua told them to wait there for "the promised gift of the Father" (Acts 1:4). Also, they were gathered together in one place on the same *day*, **because they were obediently observing the Feast of Weeks in Jerusalem,** as commanded by God's Torah. They met, just as they always had over the years, to pray and sing the songs of *that holy day*. What a reward they received while celebrating that special Sabbath during that particular year!

Other themes of the month Sivan

God's salvation on a physical level, too, persists in the month Sivan. **On Sivan 23, Esther and Mordechai sent copies of the king's decree** throughout his entire empire, granting the Jews the right to assemble and defend themselves (Esther 8:9). This decree saved the Jewish people from extermination.

Perhaps no greater example of God's personal revelation to the heart of an individual is that of **King David.** An ancient Jewish **tradition** holds that **David both was born, and died, on Sivan 6, Shavuot/Pentecost.** Peter's famous speech on Pentecost day makes a timely reference to **David's death** (Acts 2:29).

"It will be in the last days," says God, "that I will pour out my Spirit on all flesh... I will show wonders in the sky above, and signs on the earth beneath; blood, and fire, and billows of smoke..."

Peter's quote of the prophet Joel during his famous speech at Pentecost on Sivan 6 (Acts 2:17,19)

Sivan

In the month Sivan, the Torah was given to Moses and the people at Sinai. The believers in the book of Acts received the indwelling Holy Spirit. There were also two spiritual revivals in the Old Testament during this month, one under Asa and one under Hezekiah.

Rosh Chodesh Sivan
Head of the month of Sivan

Ezekiel prophesies downfall of Egypt *(a type of Assyria), Ezek. 31:1*

Shavuot/Pentecost
Feast of Weeks,
50th day after Firstfruits

Giving of Torah *at Sinai, Ex. 19:1-6*

Giving of Indwelling Holy Spirit *at Zion, Acts 2*

1 2 3 4 5 6 7 8 9 10 11 12 13 14 15

Worms Jews massacred by crusaders *during morning prayers, 1096*

Looting of Safed, *1834*

Traditional date of birth and death of King David

Shavuot
Israeli national holiday

Chmielnicki Massacres, *1948*

Key:

"Appointed time" or other observance established by God in scripture

Special Annual Sabbath (not necessarily falling on the seventh day of a week)

Commemorated event in Israel's history or Israeli national holiday

Event commanded by God to be observed annually

Favorable decree for Jewish protection – *provision against Haman's decree, Est. 8:9*

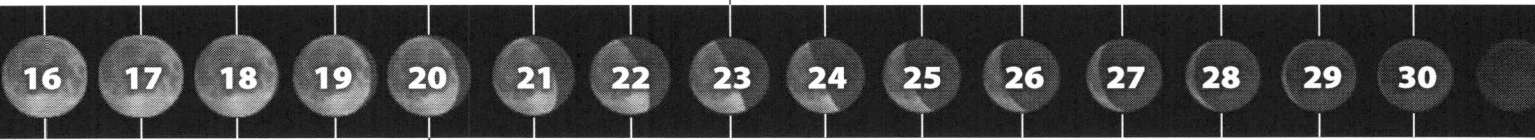

| 16 | 17 | 18 | 19 | 20 | 21 | 22 | 23 | 24 | 25 | 26 | 27 | 28 | 29 | 30 |

First Blood Libel in France *Jews are burned alive in the French town of Blois, 1171*

Scriptures using the terms *the third month* or *Sivan*

Exodus 19:1 *Giving of Torah to Moses at Sinai (context chapter 19)*

In the third month בַּחֹדֶשׁ הַשְּׁלִישִׁי after the children of Israel had gone forth out of the land of Egypt, on that same day they came into the wilderness of Sinai.

1 Chronicles 27:5 *David's civil leader – monthly duty schedule (context verses 5–6)*

The third captain of the army **for the third month** לַחֹדֶשׁ הַשְּׁלִישִׁי was Benaiah, the son of Jehoiada the priest, chief: and in his division were twenty-four thousand.

2 Chronicles 15:10 *Spiritual revival under Asa (context verses 1–15)*

So they gathered themselves together at Jerusalem **in the third month** בַּחֹדֶשׁ הַשְּׁלִישִׁי , in the fifteenth year of the reign of Asa.

2 Chronicles 31:6-7 *Spiritual revival under Hezekiah (context verses 1–8)*

The children of Israel and Judah, who lived in the cities of Judah, they also brought in the tithe of cattle and sheep, and the tithe of dedicated things which were consecrated to the LORD their God, and laid them by heaps. **In the third month** בַּחֹדֶשׁ הַשְּׁלִישִׁי they began to lay the foundation of the heaps, and finished them in the seventh month.

Esther 8:9 *A favorable decree for the protection of the Jews (context verses 1–11)*

Then the king's scribes were called at that time, **in the third month** בַּחֹדֶשׁ הַשְּׁלִישִׁי that is **the month Sivan** חֹדֶשׁ סִיוָן , on the twenty-third day of the month; and it was written according to all that Mordecai commanded to the Jews...

Ezekiel 31:1 *Prophesied downfall of Egypt*

It happened in the eleventh year, **in the third month** בַּשְּׁלִישִׁי , in the first day of the month, that the word of the LORD came to me, saying...

But Peter, standing up with the eleven, lifted up his voice, and spoke out to them, "You men of Judea, and all you who dwell at Jerusalem, let this be known to you, and listen to my words. For these aren't drunken, as you suppose, seeing it is only the third hour of the day. But this is what has been spoken through the prophet Joel:

'It will be in the last days, says God, that I will pour out my Spirit on all flesh. Your sons and your daughters will prophesy. Your young men will see visions. Your old men will dream dreams. Yes, and on my servants and on my handmaidens in those days, I will pour out my Spirit, and they will prophesy. I will show wonders in the sky above, and signs on the earth beneath; blood, and fire, and billows of smoke. The sun will be turned into darkness, and the moon into blood, before the great and glorious day of the LORD comes. It will be that whoever will call on the name of the LORD will be saved.'

"Men of Israel, hear these words! Jesus of Nazareth, a man approved by God to you by mighty works and wonders and signs which God did by Him among you, even as you yourselves know, Him, being delivered up by the determined counsel and foreknowledge of God, you have taken by the hand of lawless men, crucified and killed; Whom God raised up, having freed Him from the agony of death, because it was not possible that He should be held by it. For David says concerning Him,

'I saw the LORD always before my face, For He is on my right hand, that I should not be moved. Therefore my heart was glad, and my tongue rejoiced. Moreover my flesh also will dwell in hope; because You will not leave my soul in Hades, neither will You allow your Holy One to see decay. You made known to me the ways of life. You will make me full of gladness with Your presence.'

"Brothers, I may tell you freely of the patriarch David, that he both died and was buried, and his tomb is with us to this day..."

Acts 2:14–29

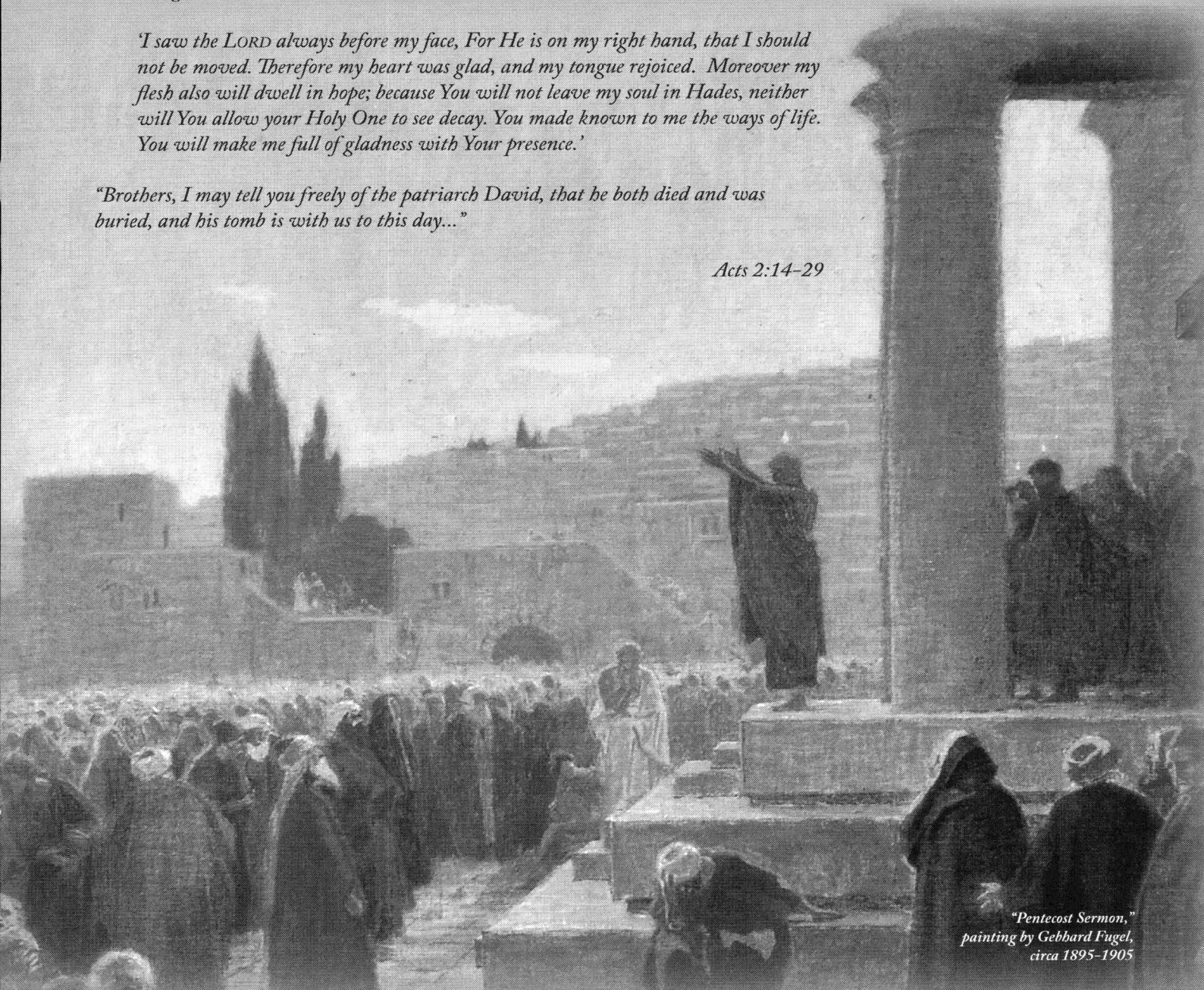

"Pentecost Sermon,"
painting by Gebhard Fugel,
circa 1895–1905

"You shall have no other gods before Me."

The words of God, Exodus 20:3

Moses Destroys the Tables of the Ten Commandments – painting by James Jacques Joseph Tissot, c. 1896–1902

Therefore, my beloved, flee from idolatry.

1 Corinthians 10:14

The Adoration of the Golden Calf – painting by Nicolas Poussin, 1633

The Siege and Destruction of Jerusalem by the Romans under the Command of Titus, 70 AD – painting by David Roberts, 1850.

The Fourth Month

The fourth month of the Biblical year is also known by its post-exilic name, **Tammuz** (pronounced *tah-MOOZ*). It corresponds to June/July in the western calendar.

Biblical themes of the month Tammuz

The theme of the month Tammuz is the tragic consequences of idolatry. Time and again in Israel's history, God used the month Tammuz prophetically as a month to discipline His beloved people because of idolatry. Each time, the LORD reluctantly employed very harsh measures as a last ditch effort, having first given warnings through His prophets (who were ignored, abused or killed). Famine, siege, and captivity were ultimately required in order to turn the people's hearts away from their spirit-killing love of idols, greed and corruption. Catastrophes resulting from idolatry or apostasy which occurred in the month Tammuz include:

- **The golden calf** and Moses' smashing of the tablets (Ex. 32)

- **Walls of Jerusalem breached by Nebuchadnezzar** on Tammuz 9, after a prolonged period of siege and famine, 587-586 BCE (2 Kings 25:1-7, Jer. 39:1-2, 52:4-6)

- **Walls of Jerusalem breached by the Roman army** on Tammuz 17 in the year 70 CE. This was the result of apostasy on the part of the Jewish religious leaders, according to Yeshua (Mat. 23:13-24:2).

The traditional "Five Tragedies" of Tammuz 17

A period of mourning – **the three weeks of sorrow** – is held each year by observant Jews, beginning with the **Fast of the 17th of Tammuz** and culminating with the Ninth of Av. Jewish tradition lists **five tragedies** which are believed to have occurred on Tammuz 17: Moses broke the tablets at Sinai; the daily offerings in the First Temple were suspended because of the siege of Jerusalem; Jerusalem's walls were breached prior to the destruction of the Second Temple in 70 CE; General Apostamos burned a Torah scroll; and an idolatrous image was placed in the Holy Temple.

Why "Tammuz"?

It is significant that this month is named after a Sumerian/Babylonian god. *Tammuz* was the consort of the goddess Ishtar. In ancient culture, he represented the spirit of spring vegetation and descended into Hades every year in the fourth month during the heat of summer. Idol worshippers, even some in Israel, held a period of "mourning for Tammuz." God called this idolatrous practice an "abomination" (Ezek. 8:14-15). Since God's people insisted on mourning false gods during the month Tammuz, it may have seemed to Him a fitting month to cause them to mourn over the real catastrophes He brought in response to their idolatry. Rabbinic tradition says that the name *Tammuz* was deliberately retained for this month as a reminder of God's judgment for idolatry.

> *But they mocked God's messengers, despised His words and scoffed at His prophets until the wrath of the LORD was aroused against His people and there was no remedy.*
>
> *2 Chronicles 36:16*

Tammuz

The theme of this month is catastrophe as a result of idolatry / apostasy. Moses smashed the tablets during this month (cf. Ex. 24:16,18 and Ex. 32). The walls of Jerusalem were breached <u>twice</u> in history, during Tammuz.

Rosh Chodesh Tammuz
Head of the month of Tammuz

Ezekiel's "wheels" vision *while in captivity, Ezek. 1:1-6*

Walls of Jerusalem breached by Nebuchadnezzar *following prolonged siege and famine, 586 BCE, 2 Kings 25:1-7, Jer. 39:1-2, 52:4-6*

1 2 3 4 5 6 7 8 9 10 11 12 13 14 15

Original Fast of Tammuz –
Initial day of mourning over the breach by Nebuchadnezzar and subsequent captivity by the Babylonians. This fast day was later consolidated with the 17th of Tammuz, after the Roman army breached the walls again in 70 CE, on Tammuz 17.

Key:

"Appointed time" or other observance established by God in scripture

Special Annual Sabbath (not necessarily falling on the seventh day of a week)

Commemorated event in Israel's history or Israeli national holiday

Event commanded by God to be observed annually

16　17　18　19　20　21　22　23　24　25　26　27　28　29

Shivah Asar b'Tammuz, *Fast of the 17th of Tammuz, a man-made fast beginning the "Three Weeks of Sorrow" and commemorating the Five Tragedies listed below (some of which are traditional, some historical):*

Golden calf idolatry; smashing of the tablets by Moses *(traditional date)*

Daily sacrifices in the temple discontinued due to the siege by the Babylonians *(traditional date)*

Walls of Jerusalem breached by Roman army, *70 CE, historical date*

General Apostomus (Apustemus) burned the Torah, *according to tradition*

An idol was set up in the Lᴏʀᴅ's Temple by King Manasseh *(traditional date)*

Scriptures using the terms *the fourth month* or *Tammuz*

2 Kings 25:3 *Severe famine during siege of Jerusalem in 586 BCE (context verses 1–7)*

On the ninth day **of the fourth month** לַחֹדֶשׁ the famine was severe in the city, so that there was no bread for the people of the land.

1 Chronicles 27:7 *David's civil leader – monthly duty schedule*

The fourth captain **for the fourth month** לַחֹדֶשׁ הָרְבִיעִי was Asahel the brother of Joab, and Zebadiah his son after him: and in his division were twenty-four thousand.

Jeremiah 39:2 *The breach on Tammuz 9 – the fall of Jerusalem in 586 BCE (context verses 1–2)*

...in the eleventh year of Zedekiah, **in the fourth month** בַּחֹדֶשׁ הָרְבִיעִי , the ninth day of the month, a breach was made in the city...

Jeremiah 52:6 *Severe famine during siege of Jerusalem in 586 BCE (context verses 4–6)*

In the fourth month בַּחֹדֶשׁ הָרְבִיעִי , in the ninth day of the month, the famine was severe in the city, so that there was no bread for the people of the land.

Ezekiel 1:1 *Ezekiel, in captivity, receives a vision and God's words of warning to a rebellious people*

Now it happened in the thirtieth year, **in the fourth month** בָּרְבִיעִי , in the fifth day of the month, as I was among the captives by the river Chebar, that the heavens were opened, and I saw visions of God.

Ezekiel 8:14-15 *God shows Ezekiel that His people are worshipping the false god Tammuz*

Then he brought me to the door of the gate of the LORD's house which was toward the north; and see, there sat the women weeping for **Tammuz** הַתַּמּוּז. Then he said to me, "Have you seen this, son of man? You shall again see yet greater abominations than these."

Zechariah 8:19 *Four man-made fasts will one day be turned into feasts (context verses 18–23)*

Thus says the LORD of Armies: "The fasts of **the fourth** הָרְבִיעִי , fifth, seventh, and tenth months shall be for the house of Judah joy and gladness, and cheerful feasts. Therefore love truth and peace."

"The Golden Calf," painting by James Jacques Joseph Tissot, c.1896–1902

Furthermore, all the leaders of the priests and the people became more and more unfaithful, following all the detestable practices of the nations and defiling the temple of the LORD, which He had consecrated in Jerusalem. The LORD, the God of their ancestors, sent word to them through His messengers again and again, because He had pity on His people and on His dwelling place.   But they mocked God's messengers, despised His words and scoffed at His prophets until the wrath of the LORD was aroused against His people and there was no remedy.

He brought up against them the king of the Babylonians, who killed their young men with the sword in the sanctuary, and did not spare young men or young women, the elderly or the infirm. God gave them all into the hands of Nebuchadnezzar.   He carried to Babylon all the articles from the temple of God, both large and small, and the treasures of the LORD's temple and the treasures of the king and his officials.   They set fire to God's temple and broke down the wall of Jerusalem; they burned all the palaces and destroyed everything of value there.

He carried into exile to Babylon the remnant, who escaped from the sword, and they became servants to him and his successors until the kingdom of Persia came to power.   The land enjoyed its sabbath rests; all the time of its desolation it rested, until the seventy years were completed in fulfillment of the word of the LORD spoken by Jeremiah.

2 Chronicles 36:14–21, NIV

The Chaldees Destroy the Brazen Sea [occurring in the month of Av, 586 BCE] – painting by James Jacques Joseph Tissot, c. 1896–1902

"Truly I tell you, not one stone here will be left on another."

Jesus' prophecy regarding the temple – Matthew 24:2

The Destruction of the Temple of Jerusalem [occurring in the month of Av, 70 CE] – painting by Francesco Hayes, 1867

The Fifth Month

The fifth month of the Biblical year is also known by its post-exilic name, **Av** (pronounced *ahv*). It corresponds to July/August in the western calendar.

Biblical themes of the month Av

The month of Av is about the destruction of the temple. Which temple? Both. That's right. Both the **first** temple (a.k.a. "Solomon's") and the **second** temple (a.k.a. "Herod's") were destroyed on the same **date** – the **ninth of Av** – many centuries apart! God's severe judgment for Israel's idolatry and apostasy was most painfully expressed in the physical destruction of His house – His own Most Holy Place, in which His Spirit once dwelled in glory among His people.

Events which occurred in the month Av, mentioned in scripture, include:

- **The death of Aaron** on the first day of Av (Num. 33:38)

- **The destruction of the first temple and of Jerusalem**, followed by the **captivity** of Israel by the Babylonians, 586 BCE (2 Kings 25, Jer. 52)

- **Ezra's arrival in Jerusalem** after the captivity, launching a national revival among the remnant of the Jews, on the first day of Av (Ezra 7:8-9)

Historical events of the month Av

An astonishing historical fact is that **the Romans destroyed the temple** in 70 CE *on the same date* that Nebuchadnezzar destroyed the temple in 586 BCE. Some of the major historical events that occurred in Av include:

- **The destruction of the second temple** by the Romans, Av 9, 70 CE

- **Jews of England were expelled** on Av 9 in 1290 CE. (The edict remained in full force for more than three centuries.)

- **Jews of Spain were expelled** on Av 7 in 1492 CE. (In 2015, Spanish Parliament finally passed a law recognizing their descendants as Spanish.)

The saddest day in Jewish history

Because of the sadness associated with the loss of not *one*, but *two*, holy temples which God Himself held precious, the first nine days of Av are a time of mourning for traditional Jews, in commemoration of these and the other historical tragedies. (Av, being the month of the grape harvest, is also believed to be the time that the twelve spies returned from the promised land, ten of whom gave a **bad report, resulting in Israel's forty years of wandering in the desert** (Num. 13)). The climax of this mourning period is the **Ninth of Av**, a day which is termed "the saddest day in Jewish history" and a traditional **day of fasting** for observant Jews. In scripture, this man-made observance is called **"the fast of the fifth month"** (Zech. 8:19).

> *Nebuzaradan ... who served the king of Babylon, came to Jerusalem. He set fire to the temple of the LORD ... The Babylonians broke up the bronze pillars, the movable stands and the bronze sea that were at the temple of the LORD and they carried all the bronze to Babylon.*
>
> Jer. 52:12-13,17, NIV

Av

This month is about mourning: mourning the destruction of the first and second temples as well as the sins of idolatry and apostasy which necessitated such severe discipline. God's message of hope and restoration is prophesied in Ezra's return to Jerusalem on the first day of this mournful month, heralding a time of spiritual cleansing, revival and joy.

Rosh Chodesh Av
Head of the month of Av

Death of Aaron, *Num. 33:38*

Ezra and his followers arrive in Jerusalem, *returning from captivity, Ezra 7:9*

Nebuzaradan's men either depart for, or arrive at, Jerusalem in 586 BCE on Av 7, *on assignment to destroy the temple, the important buildings, the houses, and the walls of Jerusalem, which took several days to accomplish – cf. 2 Kings 25:8-10, Jer. 52:12-14. Fire is set to the temple some time between Av 7 and 10; the temple burns to complete consumption by the 10th. (Compare Jewish traditional dates listed below the graphic.)*

Ezekiel confronts Israel's elders *regarding their past unfaithfulness, Ezekiel 20:1*

1 2 3 4 5 6 7 8 9 10 11 12 13 14 15

Babylonians enter the temple, eat in it, defile it, *586 BCE, (Av 7, according to Jewish tradition)*

Jews expelled from Spain
by King Ferdinand and Queen Isabella, not permitted to "ever return," 1492 CE. (This decree overturned in 2015.)

Babylonians continue feasting and defiling the temple *(Av 8, according to Jewish tradition)*

Fire finishes consuming the temple, *586 BCE, (Av 10, according to Jewish tradition)*

AMIA Bombing *in Buenos Aires, Argentina, 1994 CE*

Tisha b'Av – "Ninth of Av" *– Day of fasting for observant Jews and culmination of the Three Weeks of Sorrow. The book of Lamentations is read on this day.*

Babylonians set fire to the temple and it burns all day long, *586 BCE, (Av 9, according to Jewish tradition)*

Fall of Betar *to the Romans, ending Bar Kochba's rebellion, 133 CE*

Romans destroy the temple, *70 CE*

Jews expelled from England *by King Edward I (Jews not permitted to return for 350 years), 1290 CE*

Key:

"Appointed time" or other observance established by God in scripture

Special Annual Sabbath (not necessarily falling on the seventh day of a week)

Commemorated event in Israel's history or Israeli national holiday

Event commanded by God to be observed annually

16 17 18 19 20 21 22 23 24 25 26 27 28 29 30

Hebron Massacre – *67 Jews killed, 1929 CE*

Scriptures using the terms *the fifth month* or *Av*

Numbers 33:38 *The death of Aaron (cf. Numbers 20:23–29)*

Aaron the priest went up into Mount Hor at the commandment of the LORD, and died there, in the fortieth year after the children of Israel were come out of the land of Egypt, **in the fifth month** בַּחֹדֶשׁ הַחֲמִישִׁי , on the first day of the month.

2 Kings 25:8 *Destruction of the temple and Jerusalem; the captivity begins (context verses 1–10)*

Now in the fifth month וּבַחֹדֶשׁ הַחֲמִישִׁי , on the seventh day of the month, which was the nineteenth year of king Nebuchadnezzar, king of Babylon, came Nebuzaradan the captain of the guard, a servant of the king of Babylon, to Jerusalem.

1 Chronicles 27:8 *David's civil leader – monthly duty schedule*

The fifth captain **for the fifth month** לַחֹדֶשׁ הַחֲמִישִׁי was Shamhuth the Izrahite: and in his division were twenty-four thousand.

Ezra 7:8-9 *Ezra and his followers arrive in Jerusalem; revival to begin (context verses 1–10)*

He came to Jerusalem **in the fifth month** בַּחֹדֶשׁ הַחֲמִישִׁי , which was in the seventh year of the king. For on the first day of the first month he began to go up from Babylon; and on the first day **of the fifth month** לַחֹדֶשׁ הַחֲמִישִׁי he came to Jerusalem, according to the good hand of his God on him.

Jeremiah 1:3 *A reference to the time that Israel went into exile (context verses 1–3)*

It [the word of the LORD] came also in the days of Jehoiakim the son of Josiah, king of Judah, to the end of the eleventh year of Zedekiah, the son of Josiah, king of Judah, to the carrying away of Jerusalem captive **in the fifth month** בַּחֹדֶשׁ הַחֲמִישִׁי .

"The Flight of the Prisoners" – painting depicting the Babylonians leading Israel out of Jerusalem and into captivity in the month of Av, 586 BCE. By James Jacques Joseph Tissot, c. 1896-1902

Jeremiah 28:1 *False prophecy of Hananiah (context verses 1–17)*

It happened the same year, in the beginning of the reign of Zedekiah king of Judah, in the fourth year, **in the fifth month** בַּחֹדֶשׁ הַחֲמִישִׁי , that Hananiah the son of Azzur, the prophet, who was of Gibeon, spoke to me in the house of the LORD, in the presence of the priests and of all the people...

Jeremiah 52:12 *Description of the destruction of the temple (context verses 12–14)*

Now in the fifth month וּבַחֹדֶשׁ הַחֲמִישִׁי , in the tenth day of the month, which was the nineteenth year of king Nebuchadnezzar, king of Babylon, came Nebuzaradan the captain of the guard, who stood before the king of Babylon, into Jerusalem...

Ezekiel 20:1 *Ezekiel confronts the elders regarding Israel's past sins (context verses 1-3, 13, 16, 21)*

It happened in the seventh year, **in the fifth month** בַּחֲמִשִׁי , the tenth day of the month, that certain of the elders of Israel came to inquire of the LORD, and sat before me.

Zechariah 7:3-5 *The people inquire if they should continue their man-made fast (context verses 1-7)*

... to speak to the priests of the house of the LORD of Armies, and to the prophets, saying, "Should I weep **in the fifth month** בַּחֹדֶשׁ הַחֲמִשִׁי , separating myself, as I have done these so many years?" Then the word of the LORD of Armies came to me, saying, "Speak to all the people of the land, and to the priests, saying, 'When you fasted and mourned **in the fifth** בַּחֲמִישִׁי and in the seventh month for these seventy years, did you at all fast to Me, really to Me?'"

Zechariah 8:19 *The man-made fast of the Ninth of Av will become a joyful time (context verses 18-23)*

Thus says the LORD of Armies: "The fasts of the fourth, **fifth** הַחֲמִישִׁי, seventh, and tenth months shall be for the house of Judah joy and gladness, and cheerful feasts. Therefore love truth and peace."

"The Conquest of Jerusalem by Emperor Titus" – painting depicting the Roman army destroying Jerusalem on Av 9, 70 CE. By Nicolas Poussin, 1638

אנכי יהוה

לא יהוה

לא תשא א

זכור את יום

לא תרצח

לא ת

לא תגנב

לא תענה

לא תחמד

*You shall seek Me,
and find Me,
when you shall
search for Me with
all your heart.*
– Jer. 29:13

I will seek him whom my soul loves.
– Songs 3:2

*For thus says the LORD
to the house of Israel:
"Seek Me, and you will live."*
– Amos 5:4

*Repent therefore,
and turn again,
that your sins may
be blotted out, so
that there may
come times of
refreshing from the
presence of
the LORD.*
– Acts 3:19

*God, you are my God.
I will earnestly seek you.*
– Psalm 63:1

*My beloved is mine,
and I am his.*
– Songs 2:16

The voice of one crying in the wilderness, "Make ready the way of the LORD! Make his paths straight!" *– Mark 1:3*

The Sixth Month

The sixth month of the Biblical year is also known by its post-exilic name, **Elul** (pronounced *eh-LOOL*). It corresponds to August/September.

Biblical theme – repairing the breach

The month of Elul is a month of preparation and a call to repentance. Being the month prior to the seventh month, which contains the most holy day of the year (the Day of Atonement or *Yom Kippur*), Elul is considered the *month of preparation*. While many physical preparations may be required for the upcoming series of holy days in the seventh month, of utmost importance is the *preparation of the heart*.

The first day of Elul begins a **forty day countdown to the Day of Atonement**, and therefore Elul is a time of *searching* and *repentance*. This *searching* includes both searching our heart for areas of sin and rebellion which need forgiveness, and seeking God Himself, for a closer communion with Him. *Repentance* means *returning* – *turning* away from sin and *turning* back to God – thus **repairing the breach in our relationship with Him.**

A very special event which occurred in the month Elul which is mentioned in scripture is the word of the LORD coming to Haggai, which stirred up the spirit of the people to **rebuild the LORD's house** – a wonderful revival and "return of the hearts" of the people. What a picture of God's restorative forgiveness: calling His people to **repair** His temple, even though it was their sin that caused it to be destroyed.

Nehemiah and the remnant also **finished rebuilding the walls of Jerusalem** in Elul.

Elul follows on the heels of Tammuz and Av – two months of crushing punishment and disastrous tragedy due to idolatry and apostasy. The sixth month symbolizes opportunity for *repentance, return, renewal, repair* – seeking God's atonement.

Traditional views on the month Elul

Jewish tradition holds that, after the sin of the golden calf, Moses ascended again to Mount Sinai on Elul 1, stayed forty days while God wrote on the second set of tablets and revealed His Torah, and then descended from the mountain on Tishri 10, the Day of Atonement. God's forgiving restoration in this situation was astonishing.

Another beautiful tradition comes from the Hebrew spelling of *Elul*. It is also the abbreviation of the Hebrew for "My beloved is mine, and I am his." Jewish tradition says this phrase expresses the marriage between God and God's people (His Bride).

The shofar call to return, repent and repair

The month Elul is a special month, because observant Jews and Messianic believers will blow the *shofar* (ram's horn) *every day of the month* which is not a Sabbath. Its wailing sound is a "wake-up call" to the heart: **return, repent and repair!** The spirals of the shofar are visual reminders to *bend in humble repentance, turn* and *return.*

Come, and let us return to the LORD; for He has torn us to pieces, and He will heal us; He has injured us, and He will bind up our wounds.

Hosea 6:1

Return, you backsliding children; I will heal your backsliding. "Behold, we have come to You; for You are the LORD our God."

Jeremiah 3:22

Elul

Elul is the month of preparation for the coming month of Tishri, which contains the High Holy Days. Therefore, this month is about repentance – repairing the breach in our relationships with God and each other – and seeking God. It was in the month Elul – in two different periods of history – that God commanded a renewed effort to rebuild the temple (c. 520 BCE), and brought the rebuilding of the walls of Jerusalem to completion (c. 335 BCE).

Rosh Chodesh Elul
Head of the month of Elul

The command of the LORD comes through Haggai to renew the effort to rebuild God's temple *Haggai 1:1-15*

The word of the LORD comes to Ezekiel about widespread idolatry in Israel and the future destruction of the first temple *Ezekiel chapters 8 and 9*

| 1 | 2 | 3 | 4 | 5 | 6 | 7 | 8 | 9 | 10 | 11 | 12 | 13 | 14 | 15 |

Moses ascends Sinai for a third period of forty days, to receive the second set of tablets *(on this date, according to Jewish tradition)*

Forty Days of Teshuvah (Repentance) begin
The 40-day countdown to Yom Kippur (the Day of Atonement) begins today, with a sounding of the shofar (ram's horn) on each day of Elul, except for Sabbaths

Key:

"*Appointed time*" *or other observance established by God in scripture*

Special Annual Sabbath (not necessarily falling on the seventh day of a week)

Commemorated event in Israel's history or Israeli national holiday

Event commanded by God to be observed annually

The Lᴏʀᴅ stirs up the spirits of the people to work on rebuilding His temple *Haggai 1:14-15*

Rebuilding of the walls of Jerusalem completed *Nehemiah 6:15*

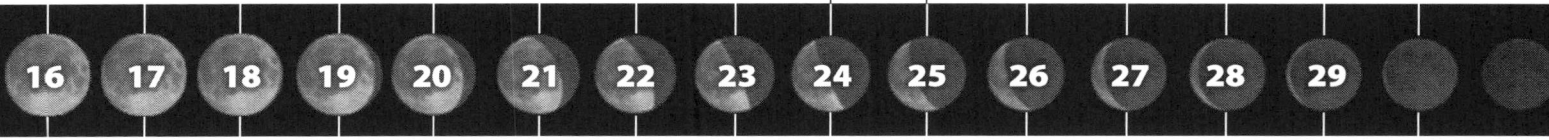

16 17 18 19 20 21 22 23 24 25 26 27 28 29

Scriptures using the terms *the sixth month* or *Elul*

1 Chronicles 27:9 *David's civil leader – monthly duty schedule*

The sixth captain **for the sixth month** לַחֹדֶשׁ הַשִּׁשִּׁי was Ira the son of Ikkesh the Tekoite: and in his division were twenty-four thousand.

Nehemiah 6:15 *Rebuilding of the walls of Jerusalem completed*

So the wall was finished in the twenty-fifth day **of Elul** לֶאֱלוּל , in fifty-two days.

Ezekiel 8:1 *Word of the LORD to Ezekiel prophesying the destruction of the temple (context chapters 8–9)*

It happened in the sixth year, **in the sixth month** בַּשִּׁשִּׁי , in the fifth day of the month, as I sat in my house, and the elders of Judah sat before me, that the hand of Adonai the LORD fell there on me.

Haggai 1:1 *God's command comes through Haggai to work on the LORD's house (context verses 1–15)*

In the second year of Darius the king, **in the sixth month** בַּחֹדֶשׁ הַשִּׁשִּׁי , in the first day of the month, the Word of the LORD came by Haggai, the prophet, to Zerubbabel, the son of Shealtiel, governor of Judah, and to Joshua, the son of Jehozadak, the high priest, saying...

Haggai 1:14-15 *People's spirits are stirred to work on the LORD's house (context verses 1–15)*

The LORD stirred up the spirit of Zerubbabel, the son of Shealtiel, governor of Judah, and the spirit of Joshua, the son of Jehozadak, the high priest, and the spirit of all the remnant of the people; and they came and worked on the house of the LORD of Armies, their God, in the twenty-fourth day of the month, **in the sixth month** בַּשִּׁשִּׁי , in the second year of Darius the king.

The Shofar Call to Repentance and to Repair the Breach

"Cry aloud, don't spare, lift up your voice like a shofar, and declare to My people their disobedience,
and to the house of Jacob their sins. Yet they seek Me daily, and delight to know My ways:
as if they were a nation that did righteousness, and didn't forsake the ordinance of their God,
they ask of Me righteous judgments; as if they delight to draw near to God.
'Why have we fasted,' say they, 'and You don't see?
Why have we afflicted our soul, and You take no knowledge?'
Behold, in the day of your fast you find pleasure, and exact all your labors.
Behold, you fast for strife and contention, and to strike with the fist of wickedness:
you don't fast this day so as to make your voice to be heard on high.
Is such the fast that I have chosen? the day for a man to afflict his soul?
Is it to bow down his head as a rush, and to spread sackcloth and ashes under him?
Will you call this a fast, and an acceptable day to The LORD?
Isn't this the fast that I have chosen: to release the bonds of wickedness,
to undo the bands of the yoke, and to let the oppressed go free, and that you break every yoke?
Isn't it to distribute your bread to the hungry, and that you bring the poor who are cast out to your house?
When you see the naked, that you cover him; and that you not hide yourself from your own flesh?
Then your light shall break forth as the morning, and your healing shall spring forth speedily;
and your righteousness shall go before you; the glory of The LORD shall be your rear guard.
Then you shall call, and The LORD will answer; you shall cry, and He will say, 'Here I am.'
If you take away from the midst of you the yoke, the putting forth of the finger, and speaking wickedly;
and if you draw out your soul to the hungry, and satisfy the afflicted soul:
then your light shall rise in darkness, and your obscurity be as the noonday;
and The LORD will guide you continually, and satisfy your soul in dry places, and make strong your bones;
and you shall be like a watered garden, and like a spring of water, whose waters don't fail.
Those who shall be of you shall build the old waste places;
you shall raise up the foundations of many generations; and you shall be called
The Repairer of the Breach,
The Restorer of Paths to Dwell in."

– The words of the LORD, Isaiah 58

The Day of
The Shout...
(Feast of Trumpets)

The Translation
of Believers
("Rapture")

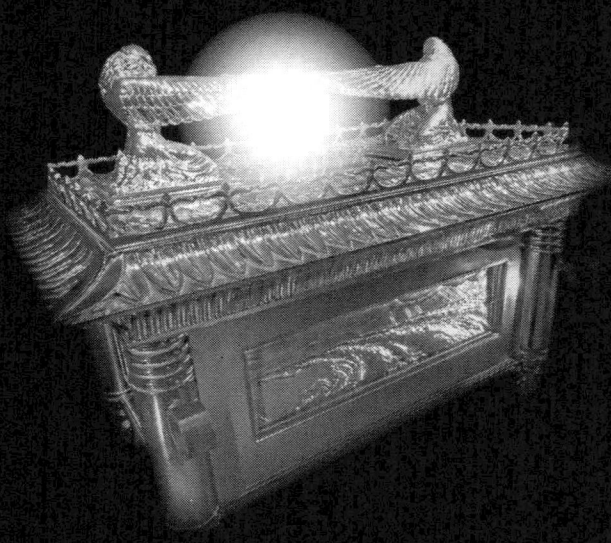

The Day of
Atonement...

The Atonement
of All Israel
(the Believing
Remnant)

The Feast of Booths...
(Tabernacles)

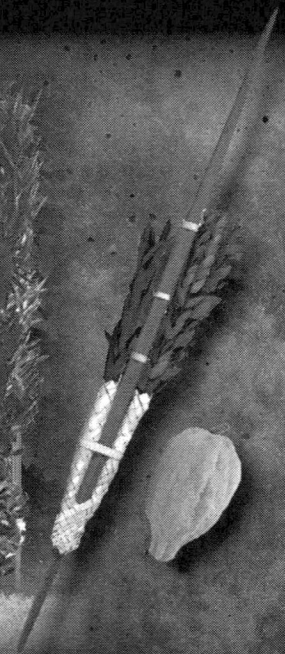

The Millennial
Kingdom
of Messiah

The Seventh Month

The seventh month of the Biblical year is also known by its pre-exilic name, **Etanim** (pronounced *ay-tah-NEEM*) or its post-exilic name (which has two variant spellings in Hebrew): **Tishrei** (pronounced *tish-ray*) or **Tishri** (pronounced *tish-ree*). It corresponds to September/October in the western calendar.

Biblical themes of the month Tishri

The month of Tishri contains the most holy day of the Biblical year, along with several other significant holy days. The holy days in Tishri, occurring as they do in the *seventh* month in the *fall*, are all prophetic of events *yet to be fulfilled by Jesus.*

- **The Feast of Trumpets** (*Yom Teruah*, the *Day of the Shout/Blast*) is a special annual Sabbath that occurs on Tishri 1 (Lev. 23:24, Num. 29:1). It is a prophetic symbol of the *translation of believers*, also called the "rapture" (1 Thess. 4:16-17).

- **The Day of Atonement** (*Yom Kippur*) occurs on Tishri 10 (Lev. 23:27-28, 16:29), **the only day of fasting that is commanded by God as a permanent statute** for Israel. It is a special annual Sabbath as well. This day is a prophetic symbol of the future atonement of all Israel in our Messiah Yeshua (Rom. 11:26). The only day the high priest entered the Holy of Holies, this day is the holiest day of the year.

- **The Feast of Booths** (*Sukkot*, Tabernacles) is a seven-day feast that begins on Tishri 15, followed by an additional eighth day of assembly (Lev. 23:34-36). The first and eighth days are special annual Sabbaths. This feast is a prophetic symbol of Messiah tabernacling with us – the thousand year, worldwide reign of Jesus, which He will establish after His second coming.

Traditional views on events in Tishri

- **The Head of the Year** (*Rosh HaShanah*) – another name used for the first day of Tishri. Ancient Mesopotamian cultures observed Tishri as the first month of the year. One reason that Tishri was the used as the first month was that most harvesting was completed at this time, so tithes, tributes or taxes were exacted and paid then. To this day, the Jewish *civil calendar* continues to use Tishri as the beginning of its *fiscal year for tithes*, much in the same way that businesses may assign any given month to be the start of their own fiscal years. However, the Jewish *religious calendar* still observes Nisan/Abib as the start of the *religious* year.

- **Atonement** – Over time, traditional Jewish views on atonement have changed from the Biblical understanding that sin must be atoned for by blood sacrifice, to the widespread modern understanding that fasting and prayer on Yom Kippur will merit a more "favorable" year. *The Ten Days of Awe* (between Rosh HaShanah and Yom Kippur) are set apart for prayer, repentance, and giving to charity, all three of which are believed by many Jews to be sufficient for an "annual cleansing" of sin. (This belief is in opposition to what gentile Christians and Messianic Jews believe.)

- **Fast of Gedaliah** *(Tzom Gedaliah)* – In 2 Kings 25:25-26 and Jeremiah 41, we read about the assassination of a governor of Judah named Gedaliah. His murder brought about the end of Jewish self-rule after the Babylonian conquest, and thousands more Jews were killed. The rabbis instituted a man-made fast in Tishri to mourn this event. It is this man-made fast that God says will someday be turned into a day of rejoicing (Zechariah 8:19).

> *But Messiah came as a high priest...through the greater and more perfect tabernacle not made with human hands... nor by means of the blood of goats and calves, but by His own blood He entered into the Holy of Holies, once for all, thus obtaining eternal redemption.*
>
> *Hebrews 9:11-12*

Tishri / Etanim

Mentions of Tishri's "appointed times of the LORD" may be found in the New Testament. Jesus is described observing the Feast of Tabernacles in John 7. At least as late as 80 to 100 CE, more than 40 years after the resurrection, the fast of the Day of Atonement was still being observed by believers in Jesus, as shown by Luke's use of the shorthand phrase "The Fast" in Acts 27:9. Luke's casual use of this well-known synonym for Yom Kippur reveals his own intimacy with this appointed time. This phrase also reveals that Luke was certain his reader, Theophilus, would know that "The Fast" referred to Tishri 10, the Day of Atonement. Gentile believers in Jesus (as well as Jewish ones) continued observing God's appointed times for hundreds of years after Jesus' resurrection, according to the writings of both Eusebius and Constantine.

Yom Teruah *"Day of the Shout/Blast" (Feast of Trumpets), a special annual Sabbath, Lev. 23:24, Num. 29:1 Symbolic of the Translation of Believers, 1 Thess. 4:16-17*

Rosh Chodesh Tishri *Head of the month of Tishri*

Ezra brings the Torah before the people, *the people weeping as they listen, Neh. 8:2*

Burnt offerings renewed, *even before the foundation of the temple was laid, Ezra 3:6*

Yom Kippur *"Day of Atonement" (Lev. 23:27-28, 16:29) a special annual Sabbath and fast day commanded by God. Symbolic of "all Israel being saved," Rom. 11:26*

"The Fast" *mentioned by Luke in Acts 27:9*

Dedication of Solomon's temple *begins, 2 Chron. 7:9*

First Day of Sukkot *"Booths/Tabernacles" (Lev. 23:34-36). A special annual Sabbath, beginning a seven-day feast which concludes with an additional eighth day. Symbolic of the future millennial kingdom reign of the Messiah.*

All Israel attends the feast at Solomon's new temple *2 Chronicles 5:3*

Yeshua attends Sukkot *in Jerusalem, John 7*

1 2 3 4 5 6 7 8 9 10 11 12 13 14 15

Yom Kippur *Israeli national holiday*

Moses returns from his final trip to Mt. Sinai *with the second set of tablets and a message of forgiveness for the sin of the golden calf (on this date, according to Jewish tradition)*

Rabbi Akiva tortured and executed *by the Romans in the wake of the Bar Kochba rebellion, 135 CE*

Fast of Gedaliah *(Tzom Gedaliah), a man-made fast in memory of the thousands of lives lost after Gedaliah's assassination, circa 582 BCE (2 Kings 25:25-26, Jer. 41). Also called "The Fast of the Seventh Month" (Zech. 8:19).*

Days of Awe *begin, continuing through Yom Kippur*

Rosh HaShanah *(Head of the Year) First day of the first month of the Jewish Civil Year; the head of the fiscal year for tithing. Israeli national holiday.*

First Day of Sukkot - *Israeli national holiday. Also, the seven days of Sukkot (chol ha-moed) are often non-working days for schools, government offices, and certain businesses in Israel. Families build temporary booths (sukkot) outdoors and spend time eating and/or sleeping in them. Religious Jews also wave the "Four Species" of the lulav and etrog (branches and fruit of certain trees) as God commanded in the Bible (Lev. 23:40).*

Key:

[icon]	*"Appointed time" or other observance established by God in scripture*
[icon]	*Special Annual Sabbath (not necessarily falling on the seventh day of a week)*
[icon]	*Commemorated event in Israel's history or Israeli national holiday*
[icon]	*Event commanded by God to be observed annually*

Eighth Day of Assembly *"Shemini Atzeret" (Lev. 23:36). A special annual Sabbath of assembly held the day after the conclusion of the seven-day feast of Tabernacles. Also called "the Last Great Day."* [icons]

Yeshua loudly proclaims He is the source of living water, *at the temple, on "the last and greatest day" of the feast, John 7:37-39*

Word of the LORD comes to Haggai *regarding the glory of the former temple as compared to the latter, Haggai 2:1-3*

Solomon sends all the people home *full of joy, following the dedication of the new temple and the feast of Tabernacles, 2 Chron. 7:10*

| 16 | 17 | 18 | 19 | 20 | 21 | 22 | 23 | 24 | 25 | 26 | 27 | 28 | 29 | 30 |

Water Drawing Ceremony – *each day of Sukkot, in temple times, a joyful ceremony was held in which water was drawn from the Pool of Siloam in the City of David and carried up the Jerusalem pilgrim road to the temple. Tens of thousands of people sang songs of praise to God, played loud instruments, and danced with torches (Mishnah, Tractate Sukkah). It was in this context that Jesus proclaimed He was the source of living water.*

Shemini Atzeret - (Eighth Day of Assembly), *Israeli national holiday. Also called* **Simchat Torah** *(Rejoicing in the Torah), a joyful occasion in which the Torah scroll is taken out, read, and rolled back to its beginning place at Genesis 1:1* [icon]

Scriptures using the terms *the seventh month, Tishri / Tishrei* or *Etanim*

Leviticus 16:29 *God commands a fast and special Sabbath on Tishri 10, an eternal statute*

It shall be a statute to you forever: **in the seventh month** בַּחֹדֶשׁ הַשְּׁבִיעִי , on the tenth day of the month, you shall afflict your souls, and shall do no kind of work, the native-born, or the stranger who lives as a foreigner among you...

Leviticus 23:23-25 *God commands the Day of Trumpets to be a special Sabbath on Tishri 1*

The Lord spoke to Moses, saying, "Speak to the children of Israel, saying, '**In the seventh month** בַּחֹדֶשׁ הַשְּׁבִיעִי , on the first day of the month, shall be a solemn rest to you, a memorial of blowing of trumpets, a holy convocation. You shall do no regular work; and you shall offer an offering made by fire to the Lord.'"

Leviticus 23:27-28 *God commands the Day of Atonement to be a special Sabbath and fast day, Tishri 10*

"However on the tenth day **of this seventh month** לַחֹדֶשׁ הַשְּׁבִיעִי is the day of atonement: it shall be a holy convocation to you, and you shall afflict yourselves; and you shall offer an offering made by fire to the Lord. You shall do no kind of work in that same day; for it is a day of atonement, to make atonement for you before the Lord your God."

Leviticus 23:33-35 *God sets the first day of the Feast of Tabernacles as a special Sabbath, Tishri 15*

The Lord spoke to Moses, saying, "Speak to the children of Israel, and say, 'On the fifteenth day **of this seventh month** לַחֹדֶשׁ הַשְּׁבִיעִי is the feast of tabernacles for seven days to the Lord. On the first day shall be a holy convocation: you shall do no regular work."

Leviticus 23:39 *God sets the first and eighth days of Tabernacles as special Sabbaths, Tishri 15 & 22*

"So on the fifteenth day **of the seventh month** לַחֹדֶשׁ הַשְּׁבִיעִי , when you have gathered in the fruits of the land, you shall keep the feast of the Lord seven days: on the first day shall be a solemn rest, and on the eighth day shall be a solemn rest."

Leviticus 23:41-43 *God commands that the Feast of Tabernacles (Booths) be kept forever*

"You shall keep it a feast to the LORD seven days in the year: it is a statute forever throughout your generations; you shall keep it **in the seventh month** בַּחֹדֶשׁ הַשְּׁבִיעִי . You shall dwell in booths seven days. All who are native-born in Israel shall dwell in booths, that your generations may know that I made the children of Israel to dwell in booths, when I brought them out of the land of Egypt. I am the LORD your God."

Leviticus 25:9 *The special Day of Atonement marking the jubilee year (context verses 8-12)*

"Then you shall sound the shofar [ram's horn] on the tenth day **of the seventh month** בַּחֹדֶשׁ הַשְּׁבִעִי. On the Day of Atonement you shall sound the shofar throughout all your land."

Numbers 29:1 *God commands that Tishri 1 be a special Sabbath, the Day of Trumpets*

"**In the seventh month** וּבַחֹדֶשׁ הַשְּׁבִיעִי , on the first day of the month, you shall have a holy convocation; you shall do no servile work: it is a day of blowing of trumpets to you."

Numbers 29:7 *God commands that Tishri 10 (Day of Atonement) be a fast day and special Sabbath*

"On the tenth day **of this seventh month** לַחֹדֶשׁ הַשְּׁבִיעִי , you shall have a holy convocation; and you shall afflict your souls: you shall do no kind of work..."

Numbers 29:12 *God commands that Tishri 15 (first day of Tabernacles) be a special Sabbath*

"On the fifteenth day **of the seventh month** לַחֹדֶשׁ הַשְּׁבִיעִי you shall have a holy convocation; you shall do no servile work, and you shall keep a feast to the LORD seven days..."

1 Kings 8:2 *Solomon's newly built temple is consecrated, and the feast of Tabernacles observed therein*

All the men of Israel assembled themselves to king Solomon at the feast, in the month **Etanim** הָאֵתָנִים , which is **the seventh month** הַחֹדֶשׁ הַשְּׁבִיעִי .

2 Kings 25:25 *Ishmael kills Gedaliah*

But it happened **in the seventh month** בַּחֹדֶשׁ הַשְּׁבִיעִי , that Ishmael the son of Nethaniah, the son of Elishama, of the royal seed came, and ten men with him, and struck Gedaliah, so that he died, and the Jews and the Chaldeans that were with him at Mizpah.

2 Chronicles 5:3 *Solomon's newly built temple is consecrated, and the feast of Tabernacles observed therein*

And all the men of Israel assembled themselves to the king at the feast, which was in **the seventh month** הַחֹדֶשׁ הַשְּׁבִיעִי .

2 Chronicles 7:10 *Solomon sends the people back home after the joyful consecration and feast*

On the twenty-third day **of the seventh month** לַחֹדֶשׁ הַשְּׁבִיעִי he sent the people away to their tents, joyful and glad of heart for the goodness that the LORD had shown to David, and to Solomon, and to Israel his people.

2 Chronicles 31:6-7 *During the revival of Hezekiah's time, the people bring their tithes*

The children of Israel and Judah, who lived in the cities of Judah, they also brought in the tithe of cattle and sheep, and the tithe of dedicated things which were consecrated to the LORD their God, and laid them by heaps. In the third month they began to lay the foundation of the heaps, **and in the seventh month** וּבַחֹדֶשׁ הַשְּׁבִיעִי they finished them.

Ezra 3:1,6 *Ezra and the returned captives rebuild the altar and offer burnt offerings*

When **the seventh month** הַחֹדֶשׁ הַשְּׁבִיעִי had come, and the children of Israel were in the cities, the people gathered themselves together as one man to Jerusalem... From the first day **of the seventh month** לַחֹדֶשׁ הַשְּׁבִיעִי they began to offer burnt offerings to the LORD: but the foundation of the temple of the LORD was not yet laid.

Nehemiah 7:73 *Upon rebuilding the walls of Jerusalem, the people returned to their towns*

So the priests, and the Levites, and the porters, and the singers, and some of the people, and the Nethinim, and all Israel, lived in their cities. When **the seventh month** הַחֹדֶשׁ הַשְּׁבִיעִי had come, the children of Israel were in their cities.

Nehemiah 8:2 *The people assemble to hear the reading of the Torah by Ezra*

Ezra the priest brought the law before the assembly, both men and women, and all who could hear with understanding, on the first day **of the seventh month** לַחֹדֶשׁ הַשְּׁבִיעִי .

Nehemiah 8:14-15 *As Ezra reads the Torah, the people learn more about the Feast of Tabernacles*

They found written in the Law, which the LORD had commanded through Moses, that the Israelites were to live in temporary shelters during the festival **of the seventh month** בַּחֹדֶשׁ הַשְּׁבִיעִי and that they should proclaim this word and spread it throughout their towns and in Jerusalem: "Go out into the hill country and bring back branches from olive and wild olive trees, and from myrtles, palms and shade trees, to make temporary shelters"—as it is written.

Jeremiah 28:17 *Death of Hananiah*

So Hananiah the prophet died the same year **in the seventh month** בַּחֹדֶשׁ הַשְּׁבִיעִי.

Jeremiah 41:1 *Jeremiah recounts how Ishmael ate bread with Gedaliah before assassinating him*

Now it happened **in the seventh month** בַּחֹדֶשׁ הַשְּׁבִיעִי, that Ishmael the son of Nethaniah, the son of Elishama, of the seed royal and one of the chief officers of the king, and ten men with him, came to Gedaliah the son of Ahikam to Mizpah; and there they ate bread together in Mizpah.

Ezekiel 45:25 *God commands the princes of Israel regarding their offerings for Feast of Tabernacles*

"**In the seventh month** בַּשְּׁבִיעִי, in the fifteenth day of the month, in the feast, he will do the same the seven days; according to the sin offering, according to the burnt offering, and according to the meal offering, and according to the oil."

Haggai 2:1 *God speaks to Zerubbabel through Haggai about the former and latter temples' glory*

In the seventh month בַּשְּׁבִיעִי, in the twenty-first day of the month, the Word of the LORD came by Haggai the prophet, saying...

Zechariah 7:5 *The "fast of the seventh month" here is the Fast of Gedaliah, a man-made observance*

"Speak to all the people of the land, and to the priests, saying, 'When you fasted and mourned in the fifth **and in the seventh month** וּבַשְּׁבִיעִי for these seventy years, did you at all fast to Me, really to Me?'"

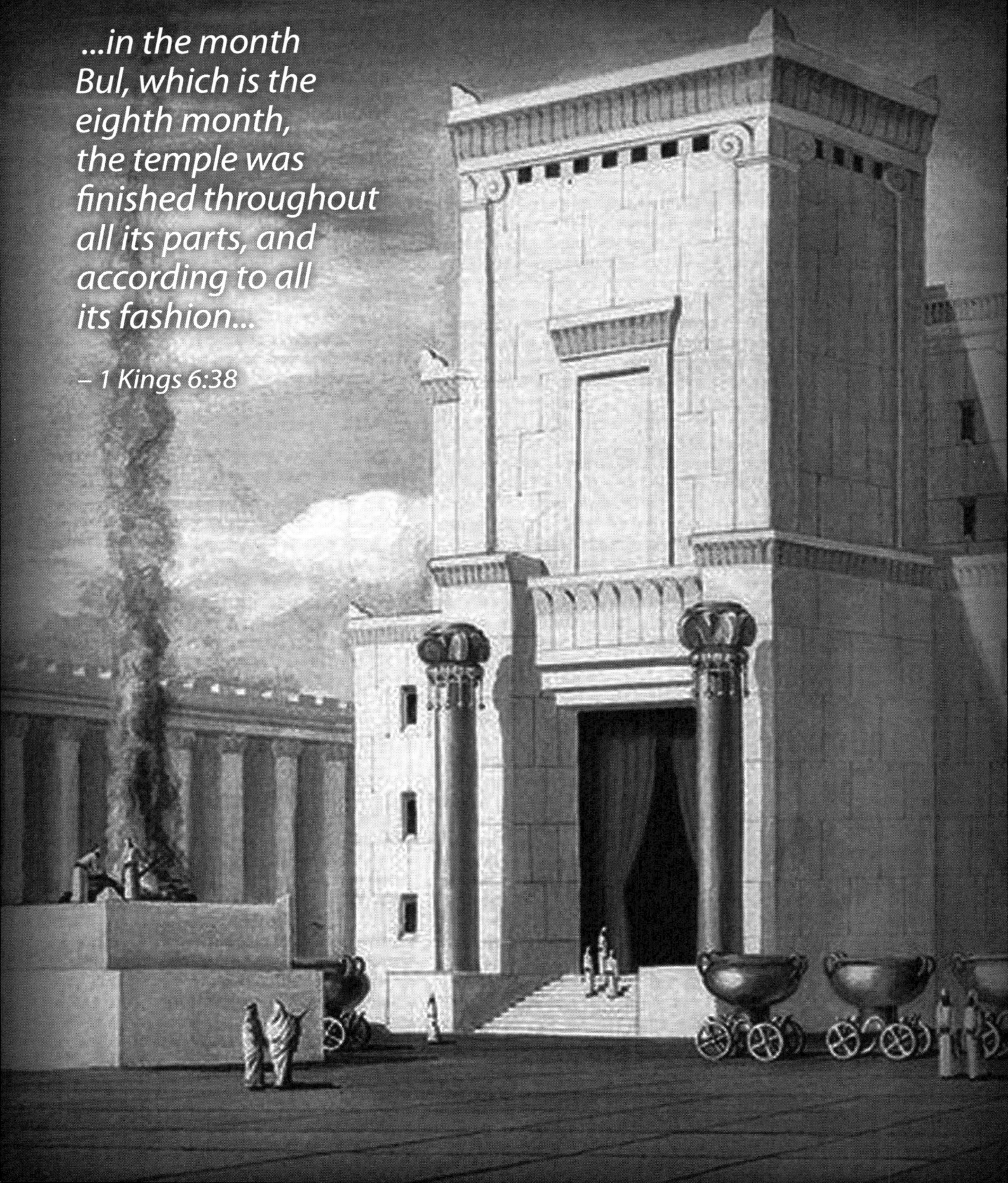

...in the month Bul, which is the eighth month, the temple was finished throughout all its parts, and according to all its fashion...

– 1 Kings 6:38

The Eighth Month

The eighth month of the Biblical year is also known by its pre-exilic name, **Bul** (pronounced *bool*) or its post-exilic name, **Marcheshvan** (pronounced *mar-chesh-vahn*). It commonly appears in its "short" form, **Cheshvan** (pronounced *chesh-vahn*). (Recall that, in Hebrew, *ch* sounds like the *ch* in *Bach* or *Loch*, not *church*.) This month corresponds to October/November in the western calendar.

Biblical themes of the month Cheshvan

The month of Cheshvan contains no special holy days, neither feasts nor fasts. Biblical events which occurred in Cheshvan include:

- **The completion of the first temple** – Solomon completed building the temple in the month Bul (Cheshvan), but, as you learned in the prior section, he did not hold a dedication ceremony until the Feast of Tabernacles in Tishri – eleven months later.

- **The institution of false religion** – Long after Solomon's death, when Israel had become a divided kingdom, Jeroboam was made king over all the tribes except Judah (which still controlled the area surrounding Jerusalem). Concerned that his people would turn against him if they attended God's feasts at Jerusalem, Jeroboam set up two golden calves, one in Bethel and one in Dan, and declared them to be gods. He then ordained a feast to these false gods on the fifteenth day of the *eighth* month – a *counterfeit* Feast of Tabernacles – telling the people it was too hard for them to travel all the way to Jerusalem in the seventh month. The people agreed, and an idolatrous cult was formed.

Traditional and historical themes of Cheshvan

Cheshvan is sometimes called the "bitter" month, not only because of the lack of holy days and the institution of formalized idolatry by Jeroboam, but because of historical events which brought suffering to Jewish people. Events occurring in Cheshvan:

- **Rachel died giving birth to Benjamin,** according to Jewish tradition

- **Yitzhak Rabin was assassinated** in 1995 on Cheshvan 12

- **Kristallnacht began** in 1938 on Cheshvan 15-16. Die Kristallnacht, the "Night of Broken Glass," was the pogrom that kicked off the Nazi campaign of terror against the Jews.

- **Inauguration of the Third Temple** – some Jewish tradition asserts that this will occur in Cheshvan. However, this temple, known as the "Tribulation Temple" to gentile Christians and Messianic Jews, will be horribly defiled after a terrible betrayal by a false Messiah, the "Antichrist." A bitter outcome, indeed.

> *Thus says the Lord of Armies: "Return to Me," says the Lord of Armies, "and I will return to you..."*
>
> The words of God to the people during the month Cheshvan, through the prophet Zechariah, Zech. 1:3

Cheshvan / Bul

During Cheshvan, Solomon completed the building of the temple, which had taken seven years to build. Jeroboam instituted a false religion of idol worship during this month.

Rosh Chodesh Cheshvan
Head of the month of Cheshvan

False feast of idol worship instituted *by Jeroboam – a counterfeit Feast of Tabernacles – 1 Kings 12*

1 2 3 4 5 6 7 8 9 10 11 12 13 14 15

Rachel dies while giving birth to Benjamin *(on this date, according to Jewish tradition)*

Yitzchak Rabin assassinated *in 1995 CE, now an Israeli national day of memorial*

Death of Matityahu (Mattathias) *the man who started the revolt of the Maccabees, 165 BCE*

Key:

"Appointed time" or other observance established by God in scripture

Special Annual Sabbath (not necessarily falling on the seventh day of a week)

Commemorated event in Israel's history or Israeli national holiday

Event commanded by God to be observed annually

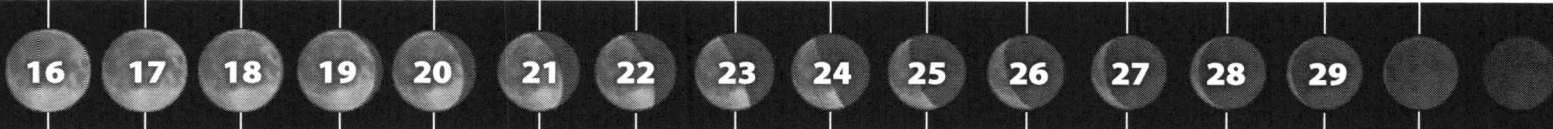

16 17 18 19 20 21 22 23 24 25 26 27 28 29

Commemoration of the removal of the defiled altar stones from the temple – *The Greeks had defiled the temple, and after the Maccabean revolt, the Jewish people were finally able to cleanse and restore the temple, 137 BCE*

Kristallnacht (Pogromnacht)
"Night of Broken Glass" – start of the Nazi terror campaign against Jews in Germany, 1938 CE. Nazis torched synagogues, vandalized or destroyed Jewish homes, schools and businesses and killed close to a hundred Jews. In the days that followed, about 30,000 Jewish men were sent to Nazi concentration camps.

Cheshvan usually has 29 days, but a thirtieth day must occasionally be added to make a full year.

Scriptures using the terms *the eighth month, Cheshvan* or *Bul*

1 Kings 6:38 *Solomon completes building the temple in the eighth month*

In the eleventh year, in the month **Bul** בּוּל , which is **the eighth month** הַחֹדֶשׁ הַשְּׁמִינִי , the temple was finished throughout all its parts, and according to all its fashion. So he was seven years in building it.

1 Kings 12:32-33 *Jeroboam establishes a counterfeit feast of Tabernacles to his golden calf idols*

Jeroboam ordained a feast **in the eighth month** בַּחֹדֶשׁ הַשְּׁמִינִי , on the fifteenth day of the month, like the feast that is in Judah, and he went up to the altar; so did he in Bethel, sacrificing to the calves that he had made: and he placed in Bethel the priests of the high places that he had made. He went up to the altar which he had made in Bethel on the fifteenth day **in the eighth month** בַּחֹדֶשׁ הַשְּׁמִינִי , even in the month which he had devised of his own heart: and he ordained a feast for the children of Israel, and went up to the altar, to burn incense.

1 Chronicles 27:11 *David's civil leader – monthly duty schedule*

The eighth captain **for the eighth month** לַחֹדֶשׁ הַשְּׁמִינִי was Sibbecai the Hushathite, of the Zerahites: and in his division were twenty-four thousand.

Zechariah 1:1-3 *God calls His people to repentance through the prophet Zechariah*

In the eighth month בַּחֹדֶשׁ הַשְּׁמִינִי , in the second year of Darius, the word of the LORD came to Zechariah the son of Berechiah, the son of Iddo, the prophet, saying, "The LORD was very displeased with your fathers. Therefore tell them: Thus says the LORD of Armies: 'Return to Me,' says the LORD of Armies, 'and I will return to you,' says the LORD of Armies."

Two kings: a study in contrasts

The righteous King Solomon built a temple to honor the LORD, in obedience to the LORD's commission. He completed it in the eighth month, but waited almost an entire year to hold its dedication ceremony, choosing to place the nation's spiritual focus upon the LORD's Feast of Tabernacles in the seventh month, the month Tishri.

"Solomon Dedicates the Temple at Jerusalem," painting by James Jacques Joseph Tissot, c. 1896–1902

The unrighteous Jeroboam, fearing loss of political power, discouraged the people from going up to Jerusalem on the fifteenth day of the seventh month to worship the LORD at His Feast of Tabernacles, because he feared he would lose their allegiance. Instead, he set up two golden calves as idols to be worshipped in two separate towns, and declared them to be Israel's gods. Jeroboam invented a false feast to be kept to these idols on the fifteenth day of the eighth month.

"Jeroboam Sacrificing to the Idols" a painting by Jean–Honoré Fragonard, 1752

...And at the temple he will set up an abomination that causes desolation, until the end that is decreed is poured out on him. — Daniel 9:27

Coin of Antiochus IV (Epiphanes). Likeness of Antiochus on front; on back, Greek inscription surrounding depiction of Zeus reads, "King Antiochus, manifestation of God, bearer of victory."

Photo courtesy of Classical Numismatic Group, Inc.

It is believed that a pig was sacrificed, its blood poured on the altar of God, 167 BCE

A statue of Zeus was said to have been set up on God's holy altar, 167 BCE

Many antichrist "types" have existed throughout history.

Nazi book burning, 1933. All books deemed "non-German" were burned, including Torah scrolls.

"So when you see standing in the holy place 'the abomination that causes desolation,' spoken of through the prophet Daniel — let the reader understand..."

— The words of Yeshua, Matthew 24:15

The Ninth Month

The ninth month of the Biblical year is also known by its post-exilic name, **Kislev** (pronounced *kis-layv*). This month corresponds to November/ December in the western calendar.

Biblical themes of the month Kislev

Scriptural events which occurred in the month **Kislev** center on **intercession by God's prophets regarding the** *desolation* **caused by** *iniquity* **and** *defilement* – contrasted against **rejection of God's word by those who despise it.** Here are some examples:

- **Ezra's prayer brings about repentance in Israel over their** *iniquity* **of intermarriage with pagans** –20th of Kislev (Ezra 10:9).

- **Nehemiah laments over the** *desolation* **of Jerusalem's ruined walls** in Kislev (Neh. 1:1)

- **Israel fasts over their** *iniquity* **as Jeremiah's scroll is read** during Kislev (Jer. 36:9). The king, **rejecting** the LORD's warning of coming judgment, **burns the scroll** (Jer. 36:22).

- **The word of God comes through Haggai, saying His temple has become** *defiled* **by the people's** *iniquity***,** which has resulted in lack of blessing – 24th of Kislev (Hag. 2:10-19)

- The word of God comes through Zechariah describing how **the pleasant land was made** *desolate* because of the people's *iniquity* – the month of Kislev (Zech. 7)

Chanukah Menorah opposite Nazi building . December, 1932. Rachel Posner, photographer. Text written on back of the photo reads, "Chanukah 5692 (1932). 'Death to Judah,' so the flag says. 'Judah will live forever,' so the light answers."

Chanukah – a prophecy of the overthrow of the Antichrist

Historical events in Kislev mirror the Biblical themes: **iniquity causing a desolation,** as well as the **rejection of God's word** by those who despise it. The celebration of **Chanukah,** meaning *dedication,* commemorates the rededication of the temple in Jerusalem after the Jews recovered it from (Syrian/Greek) Seleucid control and cleansed it of defilement in 164 BCE, in the month Kislev. The king of Syria at that time was Antiochus IV, who called himself Epiphanes (Greek: *manifest*) because he believed himself to be Zeus incarnate and desired to be worshipped. For years, he had engaged in a methodical campaign to eradicate Judaism, forbidding the reading of Torah, forcing Jews to live in a pagan manner, and modifying existing Jewish customs to tolerate idolatry. His reign of terror was all done in the name of preserving Hellenist culture. In 168/169 BCE came the last straw, when he killed the Jewish high priest, placed a statue of Zeus in his own likeness on the altar at the LORD's temple, and, according to some sources, sacrificed a pig in the temple. Jews called this event the "abomination of desecration" (see Daniel 9). **This historic king is a prophetic** *type* **of the coming Antichrist.** The recovery and cleansing of the temple was such a miraculous, Godly event that its memorial celebration, Chanukah, became an enduring tradition which was **observed by Yeshua Himself** (John 10:22-29).

The antichrist *type* repeats throughout history, a modern example being Hitler, with his Nazi campaign to eradicate Jews and Judaism. Torah scrolls and Jewish books were burned. Hitler's reign of terror, too, was done in the name of "protecting, preserving and promoting the German culture." Hitler **rejected** God's words in Genesis 12:3 and Romans 11, writing, "By defending myself against the Jew, I am fighting for the work of the Lord" (*Mein Kampf*).

Kislev

The themes of Kislev center on how iniquity creates a state of defilement which brings about desolation. Specifically, an antichrist's defiling activities will bring about an "abomination of desolation" in God's most holy place, the temple. The month is full of lament – Ezra's over Israel's sins, Nehemiah's over Jerusalem's ruined walls, the people's over God's words in Jeremiah's scroll. Following the laments, there are some victories, as the people return to God.

Rosh Chodesh Kislev
Head of the month of Kislev

Word of the LORD comes to Zechariah *regarding the "desolation of the pleasant land" as a result of the people's iniquity, Zech. 7*

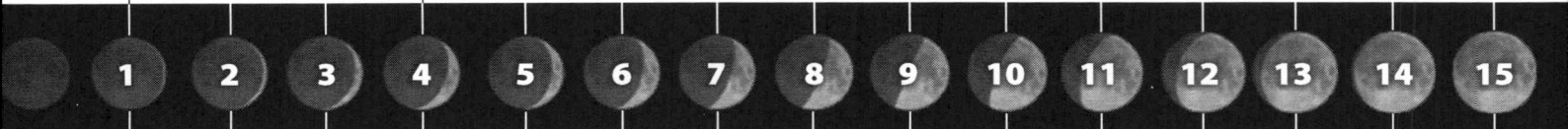

1 2 3 4 5 6 7 8 9 10 11 12 13 14 15

Ben -Gurion Day
Death of David Ben-Gurion, 1973 CE

The Greeks set up the "Abomination of Desolation" in God's temple
167 BCE (according to 1 Maccabees 1:54, an extra-Biblical writing)

Key:

"Appointed time" or other observance established by God in scripture

Special Annual Sabbath (not necessarily falling on the seventh day of a week)

Commemorated event in Israel's history or Israeli national holiday

Event commanded by God to be observed annually

Ezra confronts Israel's iniquity of intermarriage with pagans, Ezra 10:9

Word of the LORD comes to Haggai regarding the people's defilement of His temple, Haggai 2:10-19

Jesus attends Chanukah (Festival of Dedication) at the temple in Jerusalem; publicly states that He is "one with the Father," John 10:22-30

16 17 18 19 20 21 22 23 24 25 26 27 28 29 30

The Greeks make pagan sacrifices in God's temple, 167 BCE (according to 1 Maccabees 1:59, an extra-Biblical writing)

Chanukah – The Feast of the Dedication, an eight-day observance celebrating the rededication of the cleansed temple after the Greeks were driven out. At the time of Josephus, this festival was also called "The Festival of Lights." Schools in Israel closed for the eight-day holiday.

Kislev has 30 days in a regular year, but in certain years it can have only 29 days.

Scriptures using the terms *the ninth month* or *Kislev*

1 Chronicles 27:12 *David's civil leader – monthly duty schedule*

The ninth captain **for the ninth month** לַחֹדֶשׁ הַתְּשִׁיעִי was Abiezer the Anathothite, of the Benjamites: and in his division were twenty-four thousand.

Ezra 10:9 *Ezra's prayerful weeping brings about repentance over foreign wives (context verses 1–17)*

Then all the men of Judah and Benjamin gathered themselves together to Jerusalem within the three days; it was **the ninth month** חֹדֶשׁ הַתְּשִׁיעִי, on the twentieth day of the month: and all the people sat in the broad place before the house of God, trembling because of this matter...

Nehemiah 1:1 *Nehemiah laments over Jerusalem's ruined walls (context verses 1–4)*

The words of Nehemiah the son of Hacaliah. Now it happened **in the month Kislev** בְּחֹדֶשׁ כִּסְלֵו, in the twentieth year, as I was in Shushan the palace...

Jeremiah 36:9 *The people fast and pray as Jeremiah's scroll is read (context verses 1–10)*

Now it happened in the fifth year of Jehoiakim the son of Josiah, king of Judah, **in the ninth month** בַּחֹדֶשׁ הַתְּשִׁעִי, that all the people in Jerusalem, and all the people who came from the cities of Judah to Jerusalem, proclaimed a fast before the LORD.

Jeremiah 36:22-23 *The king, rejecting God's word, burns Jeremiah's scroll (context verses 11–32)*

Now the king was sitting in the winter house **in the ninth month** בַּחֹדֶשׁ הַתְּשִׁיעִי : and there was a fire in the brazier burning before him. It happened, when Jehudi had read three or four leaves, that the king cut it with the penknife, and cast it into the fire that was in the brazier, until all the scroll was consumed in the fire that was in the brazier.

Haggai 2:10,18 *The LORD's word comes to Haggai, to mark His words from the 24th of Kislev*

In the twenty-fourth day **of the ninth month** לַתְּשִׁיעִי, in the second year of Darius, the Word of the LORD came by Haggai the prophet... "Consider, please, from this day and backward, from the twenty-fourth day **of the ninth month** לַתְּשִׁיעִי, since the day that the foundation of the LORD's temple was laid, consider it."

Zechariah 7:1 *The LORD's word comes to Zechariah about the desolation of the land (context verses 1–14)*

It happened in the fourth year of king Darius that the word of the LORD came to Zechariah in the fourth day **of the ninth month** לַחֹדֶשׁ הַתְּשִׁעִי, the month of **Kislev** בְּכִסְלֵו.

"Jesus Walks in the Portico of Solomon," painting by James Jacques Joseph Tissot, c. 1886–1894

The Iniquity of Unbelief

It was the Feast of the Dedication [Chanukah] at Jerusalem. It was winter, and Jesus was walking in the temple, in Solomon's porch. The Judean [leaders] therefore came around him and said to him, "How long will you hold us in suspense? If you are the Christ, tell us plainly." Jesus answered them, "I told you, and you don't believe. The works that I do in My Father's name, these testify about Me. But you don't believe, because you are not of My sheep, as I told you. My sheep hear My voice, and I know them, and they follow Me. I give eternal life to them. They will never perish, and no one will snatch them out of My hand. My Father, who has given them to Me, is greater than all. No one is able to snatch them out of My Father's hand. I and the Father are one."

John 10:22–30

Altered detail of Nebuchadnezzar and his soldiers; from "Nebuchadnezzar Ordering the Construction of the Hanging Gardens of Babylon to Please his Consort Amyitis (Nebuchadnezzar and Sémiramis)," painting by Rene~Antoine Houasse, 1676 CE, Palace of Versailles.

"It happened in the ninth year of Zedekiah's reign,
in the tenth month, on the tenth day of the month,
that Nebuchadnezzar king of Babylon marched
against Jerusalem, he and his whole army,
and encamped outside the city
and built siege works all around it."

– 2 Kings 25:1

The Tenth Month

The tenth month of the Biblical year is also known by its post-exilic name, **Tevet** (pronounced *tay-VAYT*). This month corresponds to December/January in the western calendar.

Biblical themes of the month Tevet

Several scriptural events which occurred in the month **Tevet** show **God using Babylon as His instrument of judgment**:

- **Nebuchadnezzar and the Babylonian army march against Jerusalem to besiege it** – the 10th of Tevet (2 Kings 25:1, Jer. 39:1, 52:4; Ezekiel is commanded by God to **record the date of the siege** on the same day (Ezek. 24:1).

- **The fall of Jerusalem is reported by a refugee** on the 5th of Tevet, seventeen months after its final destruction by the Babylonians (Ezek. 33:21)

- **God tells Ezekiel that the** LORD **has set His face against Egypt** on the 12th of Tevet, (Ezek. 29:1-6) Following this prophecy, God later specifies that He intends to use *Nebuchadnezzar of Babylon* to plunder and humble Egypt (Ezek. 29:17-20).

Another important event in scripture occurred in Tevet: **Esther was selected to become the wife of King Ahasuerus** – the queen – about a hundred years after the Babylonian captivity (Esther 2:16). By this time, the Persian empire had conquered Babylon, for the LORD had eventually judged Babylon for its own sins.

Historical events in the month Tevet

- **Asara b'Tevet (The Fast of Tevet), the "Fast of the Tenth Month"** (Zech. 8:19) – throughout history, a man-made fast has been held on Tevet 10, mourning the day that Nebuchadnezzar began his siege of Jerusalem. Observant Jews still hold this day as a minor fast.

- **Jews expelled from Portugal** – Tevet 22, 1496. This was only four years after the expulsion of all Jews from Spain. The initial edict of expulsion was turned into forced conversion to Christianity in 1497. Jews were prevented from leaving the country and forced by priests to be baptized as Christians.

> *"Son of man, write this date, this very date, because the king of Babylon has set himself against Jerusalem this very day."*
>
> *The word of the* LORD *to Ezekiel on the 10th of Tevet (Ezek. 24:2)*

Tevet

Tevet is a reminder that the Lord will use foreign armies, such as Babylon, as instruments of His righteous judgment. Also during this month, Esther was made queen of an empire that God had used to judge Babylon itself.

Nebuchadnezzar *marches against Jerusalem and begins the siege, 2 Kings 25:1*

God commands Ezekiel to record the date of the siege, *Ezek. 24:1-2*

Fast of the tenth month, *a man-made fast commemorating the siege, Zech. 8:19*

Rosh Chodesh Tevet
Head of the month of Tevet

Ezra starts the investigation into intermarriages *with foreign wives, Ezra 10:16*

Man who escaped from Jerusalem *arrives and informs Ezekiel "the city has fallen," 1 year and 5 months after the final destruction of Jerusalem, Ezek. 33:21*

God tells Ezekiel to prophesy against Egypt, *as the Lord has set Himself against Egypt, Ezek. 29:1*

| 1 | 2 | 3 | 4 | 5 | 6 | 7 | 8 | 9 | 10 | 11 | 12 | 13 | 14 | 15 |

Asara b'Tevet (The Tenth of Tevet)
A minor fast day (man-made; "the fast of the tenth month"), remembering the siege of Jerusalem, still observed today by religious Jews (although not a national holiday in Israel).

Key:

"Appointed time" or other observance established by God in scripture

Special Annual Sabbath (not necessarily falling on the seventh day of a week)

Commemorated event in Israel's history or Israeli national holiday

Event commanded by God to be observed annually

16 17 18 19 20 21 22 23 24 25 26 27 28 29

First volume of the Babylonian Talmud printed in Soncino, Italy, 1483 CE. The Talmud is a massive collection of the teachings, sermons, practical applications of law, ethics, historical notes, philosophy, traditions, legends, lore, opinions and Bible commentary of thousands of Jewish scholars, dating from before Christ through the fifth century CE .

Initial edict written to expel all Jews from Portugal in 1496 CE, which was reversed when, in 1497, Jews attempting to leave the country were prevented from leaving and forced to convert to Christianity instead.

Scriptures using the terms *the tenth month* or *Tevet*

2 Kings 25:1 *Nebuchadnezzar begins the siege of Jerusalem on the 10th of Tevet*

It happened in the ninth year of [Zedekiah's] reign, **in the tenth month** בַּחֹדֶשׁ הָעֲשִׂירִי , in the tenth day of the month, that Nebuchadnezzar king of Babylon came, he and all his army, against Jerusalem, and encamped against it; and they built forts against it around it.

1 Chronicles 27:13 *David's civil leader – monthly duty schedule*

The tenth captain **for the tenth month** לַחֹדֶשׁ הָעֲשִׂירִי was Maharai the Netophathite, of the Zerahites: and in his division were twenty-four thousand.

Ezra 10:16 *Ezra begins the formal investigation into the matter of the foreign wives, 1st of Tevet*

...Ezra the priest, with certain heads of fathers' houses, after their fathers' houses, and all of them by their names, were set apart; and they sat down in the first day **of the tenth month** לַחֹדֶשׁ הָעֲשִׂירִי to examine the matter.

Esther 2:16 *Esther is chosen to be Ahasuerus' wife and queen (context verses 16–18)*

So Esther was taken to King Ahasuerus into his royal house **in the tenth month** בַּחֹדֶשׁ הָעֲשִׂירִי , which is **the month Tevet** חֹדֶשׁ טֵבֵת , in the seventh year of his reign.

Jeremiah 39:1 *Nebuchadnezzar's siege of Jerusalem on the 10th of Tevet*

Now when Jerusalem was taken, in the ninth year of Zedekiah king of Judah, **in the tenth month** בַּחֹדֶשׁ הָעֲשִׂירִי , came Nebuchadnezzar king of Babylon and all his army against Jerusalem, and besieged it.

Jeremiah 52:4 *Nebuchadnezzar's siege of Jerusalem on the 10th of Tevet*

It happened in the ninth year of [Zedekiah's] reign, **in the tenth month** בַּחֹדֶשׁ הָעֲשִׂירִי , in the tenth day of the month, that Nebuchadnezzar king of Babylon came, he and all his army, against Jerusalem, and encamped against it; and they built forts against it round about.

Ezekiel 24:1,2 *God tells Ezekiel to record the date of Nebuchadnezzar's siege of Jerusalem: Tevet 10*

Again, in the ninth year, **in the tenth month** בַּחֹדֶשׁ הָעֲשִׂירִי , in the tenth day of the month, the word of the LORD came to me, saying, "Son of man, write the name of the day, even of this same day: the king of Babylon drew close to Jerusalem this same day."

Ezekiel 29:1,2 *God tells Ezekiel His plan to permit Nebuchadnezzar to plunder Egypt*

In the tenth year, **in the tenth month** בָּעֲשִׂרִי , on the twelfth day of the month, the word of the LORD came to me, saying, "Son of man, set your face against Pharaoh king of Egypt, and prophesy against him and against all Egypt."

Ezekiel 33:21 *A person who escaped from Jerusalem brings word to Ezekiel about the fall of the city*

It happened in the twelfth year of our captivity, **in the tenth month** בָּעֲשִׂרִי , in the fifth day of the month, that one who had escaped out of Jerusalem came to me, saying, "The city has been struck."

Zechariah 8:19 *The man-made fast of the 10th of Tevet will become a joyful time (context verses 18-23)*

Thus says the LORD of Armies: "The fasts of the fourth, fifth, seventh, and **tenth** הָעֲשִׂירִי months shall be for the house of Judah joy and gladness, and cheerful feasts. Therefore love truth and peace."

"Queen Esther," painting by Edwin Long, 1877

Esther Becomes Queen

So Esther was taken to King Ahasuerus into his royal house in the tenth month, which is the month Tevet, in the seventh year of his reign. The king loved Esther more than all the women, and she obtained favor and kindness in his sight more than all the virgins; so that he set the royal crown on her head, and made her queen instead of Vashti. Then the king made a great feast for all his princes and his servants, even Esther's feast; and he proclaimed a holiday in the provinces, and gave gifts according to the king's bounty.

Esther 2:16-18

For he shall be as a tree planted by the waters,
who spreads out its roots by the river,
and shall not fear when heat comes,
but its leaf shall be green;
and shall not be anxious in the year of drought,
neither shall cease from yielding fruit.

– Jeremiah 17:8

The Eleventh Month

The eleventh month of the Biblical year is also known by its post-exilic name, **Shevat** (pronounced *sh'-VAHT*). This month corresponds to January/February in the western calendar.

Biblical themes of the month Shevat

A prominent theme of the month Shevat is **trees**. It is during this month that the **almond tree** blossoms.

The word for *almond* in Hebrew comes from a root meaning *to watch, to awaken;* the **almond tree** is among the first of the trees to "wake up" after winter dormancy in Israel. Therefore, God establishes it as a sign of watchfulness (Jer. 1:11-12). This "**watchfulness** over His word to perform it" has two meanings: watchfulness for sin, to afflict punishment – and watchfulness for obedience – to build up. "It shall happen that, as I have **watched** over them to pluck up and to break down and to overthrow and to destroy and to afflict, so will I **watch** over them to build and to plant, says the LORD" (Jer. 31:28).

The **Tree of Life** is connected with the above passages, for God declares His wisdom – His Word – to be a *tree of life* (Prov. 3:18). The *menorah* (lampstand of the temple) is a symbol of the tree of life; its general shape resembles the branching of a tree, and God commanded its oil cups to be designed in the shape of **almond blossoms** (Ex. 25:33-34, 37:19-20).

Aaron's rod miraculously budded, flowered and produced almonds overnight (Num. 17). God performed this miracle to prove that Aaron was His **chosen, anointed priest**. This was a symbol of the miraculous resurrection of Yeshua – the **chosen Anointed One, the High Priest of God**, the "Branch who was cut off" – once a dead branch, now resurrected.

Another type of Biblical tree associated with Shevat is the **myrtle**. Its Hebrew name comes from a word meaning *low, footstool*. It is a humble shrub or low-growing tree which symbolizes **God's peace and prosperity** (Isa. 55:13). The myrtle is one of the four species of the *lulav* which is waved during the Feast of Tabernacles – the symbol of millennial peace and prosperity. Zechariah's vision of "the man among the myrtles" occurred in Shevat (Zech. 1:7-17). In that vision, God said, "I will return to Jerusalem with **mercy**, and there my house will be **rebuilt**. And the measuring line will be stretched out over Jerusalem... My towns will again overflow with **prosperity**, and the LORD will again **comfort** Zion and choose Jerusalem."

Historical events in the month Shevat

The 15th of Shevat *(Tu b'Shevat)* was ordained by the rabbis as the date for calculating the beginning of the agricultural cycle for the purpose of Biblical tithes. In modern times, it is **a day for planting trees** – Israel's "Arbor Day."

Moreover the word of the LORD came to me, saying, "Jeremiah, what do you see?" I said, "I see a branch of an almond tree." Then the LORD said to me, "You have seen well; for I watch over My word to perform it."

– Jer. 1:11-12

Shevat

"Trees" is the theme of Shevat. The almond tree blossoms during this month – a symbol of God's watchfulness over His Word to perform it. The vision of the "man standing among the myrtles" occurred during Shevat – a prophecy about rebuilding, restoration, comfort, and prosperity. It was also during Shevat that Moses restated the entire Torah to the people of Israel.

Rosh Chodesh Shevat
Head of the month of Shevat

Moses restates the Torah to Israel
Deut. 1:1-4

1 2 3 4 5 6 7 8 9 10 11 12 13 14 15

Tu b'Shevat
*The Fifteenth of Shevat,
The New Year for Trees,
(Israeli "Arbor Day")
Trees are often planted in
Israel on this day.*

Key:

▣	*"Appointed time" or other observance established by God in scripture*		
♙♙	*Special Annual Sabbath (not necessarily falling on the seventh day of a week)*		
✡	*Commemorated event in Israel's history or Israeli national holiday*		
⟳	*Event commanded by God to be observed annually*		

Zechariah's vision of the man among the myrtles, *Zech. 1:7-17*

16 17 18 19 20 21 22 23 24 25 26 27 28 29 30

Antiochus V abandons his siege of Jerusalem, *sparing the city from his plans to destroy it, c. 134 BCE. In Hasmonean times, this day was celebrated as a holiday.*

Scriptures using the terms *the eleventh month* or *Shevat*

Deuteronomy 1:3 *Moses restates the Torah to the sons of Israel (context verses 1–4)*

It happened in the fortieth year, **in the eleventh month** בְּעַשְׁתֵּי עָשָׂר חֹדֶשׁ , on the first day of the month, that Moses spoke to the children of Israel, according to all that the LORD had given him in commandment to them.

1 Chronicles 27:14 *David's civil leader – monthly duty schedule*

The eleventh captain **for the eleventh month** לְעַשְׁתֵּי עָשָׂר הַחֹדֶשׁ was Benaiah the Pirathonite, of the children of Ephraim: and in his division were twenty-four thousand.

Zechariah 1:7-8 *The vision of the man standing among the myrtles comes to Zechariah on Shevat 24*

On the twenty-fourth day **of the eleventh month** לְעַשְׁתֵּי עָשָׂר חֹדֶשׁ , which is **the month Shevat** חֹדֶשׁ שְׁבָט , in the second year of Darius, the word of the LORD came to Zechariah the son of Berechiah, the son of Iddo, the prophet, saying, "I had a vision in the night, and behold, a man riding on a red horse, and he stood among the myrtle trees that were in a ravine; and behind him there were red, brown, and white horses."

The lulav, waved in worship at the Feast of Tabernacles, contains branches of the myrtle.

The vision of the man among the myrtles

"I will return to Jerusalem with mercy, and there my house will be rebuilt. And the measuring line will be stretched out over Jerusalem... My towns will again overflow with prosperity, and the LORD will again comfort Zion and choose Jerusalem."

Zechariah 1:16–17

Myrtus Communis, the myrtle of Israel. Photo by Krzysztof Golik.

He showed me a river of water of life, clear as crystal, proceeding out of the throne of God and of the Lamb, in the middle of its street. On this side of the river and on that was the tree of life, bearing twelve kinds of fruits, yielding its fruit every month. The leaves of the tree were for the healing of the nations.

Revelation 22:1-2

"Esther and Mordecai writing the letters to the Jews,"
painting by Aert de Gelder, 1675.

Mordecai wrote in the name of King Ahasuerus, and sealed it with the king's ring,
and sent letters by courier on horseback, riding on royal horses that were bred from
swift steeds. In those letters, the king granted the Jews who were in every city
to gather themselves together, and to defend their life, to destroy, to kill,
and to cause to perish, all the power of the people and province
that would assault them, their little ones and women,
and to plunder their possessions, on one day in all the provinces of King Ahasuerus,
on the thirteenth day of the twelfth month, which is the month Adar.

– Esther 8:10-12

The Twelfth Month

The twelfth month of the Biblical year is also known by its post-exilic name, **Adar** (pronounced *ah-DAR*). It corresponds to February/March in the western calendar.

Biblical themes of the month Adar

The most prominent Biblical themes of the month Adar derive from the book of Esther. In this book of the Bible, God is not referred to by name, yet His unseen hand directs every twist and turn of the plot – ingeniously – and down to the smallest detail. Indisputably, it was God Himself who miraculously saved His people from genocide in this remarkable historical event. There are many references to the words "the king" and "royal" in this book, which rabbinic and Christian commentators alike believe to be veiled references to the ultimate royal authority – **God, King of the Universe.** A major theme of Adar is **God, the Supreme King, who turns the hearts of earthly kings.**

An important theme of the book of Esther is **the contrast between the *damnation* of those who put their faith in the idolatry of Luck/Chance/Fortune (i.e., "the lot"), and the *salvation* of those who put their faith in the King of the Universe** – without Whose consent nothing is permitted to exist. "For by Him all things were created, in the heavens and on the earth, things visible and things invisible, whether thrones or dominions or principalities or powers; all things have been created through Him, and for Him" (Col. 1:16).

Haman, the villain of the book of Esther, **was a living example of the antichrist archetype**. He was lustful for the authority of the throne, became enraged when the Jew Mordecai refused to bow to him (worship him), attempted to destroy all Jews, and instead was himself destroyed. The minor feast of *Purim* commemorates the book of Esther. Because of its depiction of the antichrist's destruction, Purim is considered to be "spiritually linked" with the minor feast of Chanukah.

Scriptural events which occurred in the month **Adar**:

- **Haman's cast lot** informed him that **the Jews should be destroyed on Adar 13** (Est. 3:13). **A royal edict** countering Haman's decree **permitted Jewish self defense on Adar 13** (Est. 8:8-17). **Jewish victory** ensued (Est. 9).

- **The feast of Purim was established by Mordecai,** to be held in the month Adar (Esther 9:20-28). *Purim,* Hebrew for "lots," was the Biblical name chosen for this feast as an enduring reminder that the wicked unwisely put their faith in *lots* (luck, fortune or chance), yet God is truly the King of all.

- **King Jehoiachin was released from prison** on Adar 27, after 37 years in exile (2 Kings 25:27-30, Jer. 52:31-34). This scripture emphasizes the *turning* of the king of Babylon **to release and then honor this Jewish king above all other kings** at his table.

- **Zerubbabel's temple was completed** on Adar 3 (Ezra 6:14-16). This chapter of Ezra explains how **God** *turned* the hearts of *three* kings – Cyrus, Darius and Artaxerxes – to enable the rebuilding of His temple.

- **Ezekiel** was commanded on Adar 1 to **lament** over the coming fall of Egypt (Ezek. 32). The essence of this chapter is the fact that **no earthly king is above God's chastisement and that God may use all kings as His instruments to deliver justice.**

> *The lot is cast into the lap, but its every decision is from the LORD.*
>
> *– Proverbs 16:33*

Adar

The theme of Adar is "The King" – the Unseen King, our LORD, who turns the hearts of earthly kings in His hand, for His own purposes (Prov. 21:1). Zerubbabel's temple is completed during Adar because of God's turning of the hearts of three foreign kings. In Adar, King Jehoiachin is released from prison and honored by the king of Babylon after his heart is turned. Ezekiel is commanded in Adar to mourn for Pharaoh, King of Egypt, as God decides to use the sword of the king of Babylon to chastise Pharaoh. God turns the heart of King Ahasuerus away from Haman and toward the Jews – they are saved in the month Adar.

Rosh Chodesh Adar
Head of the month of Adar

Jews of the city of Susa *rest and rejoice with a day of feasting, Est. 9:18*

Ezekiel is commanded to lament over Pharoah the king of Egypt, *as God determines to bring "the sword of the king of Babylon" against him, Ezek. 32:1-11*

Jews of Susa continue to defend themselves *under a separate edict of King Ahasuerus, allowing an extension to the time period of Jewish defense, Est. 9:11-15*

Jews of the rural provinces *rest and rejoice with a day of feasting, Est. 9:17*

The second temple is completed *as a result of favorable edicts by Kings Cyrus, Darius and Artaxerxes, Ezra 6:14-16*

The date indicated by Haman's lot *for the destruction of the Jews (Est. 3:7-15)*

The date ordained by the decree of King Ahasuerus *for the Jews to be allowed to defend themselves, Est. 8:8-17*

Jews defend themselves against Haman and all their enemies, *Est. 9:5*

1 2 3 4 5 6 7 8 9 10 11 12 13 14 15

Jerusalem falls to Nebuchadnezzar II and Jehoiachin is captured *(on this date, according to the Babylonian Chronicles)*

Yom Nicanor
(The Day of Nicanor), the day that the Maccabees defeated Syrian general Nicanor, 161 BCE (according to 2 Maccabees 15:36, an extra-Biblical writing)

Proclamation of the Half Shekel *(during the Second Temple period) – official reminder to the people to prepare their annual offering to the temple treasury (Ex. 30:11-16)*

Ta'anit Esther *(The Fast of Esther) – a minor man-made fast from dawn until dusk on Purim eve, commemorating the three-day fast observed by the Jewish people in the book of Esther.*

Purim (celebration of the Book of Esther) *is observed on this date in most of Israel and around the world, in accordance with Esther chapter 9*

Purim *is observed on this date in certain cities in Israel which were "walled cities" in ancient times (such as Jerusalem) in accordance with Esther chapter 9*

Key:

"Appointed time" or other observance established by God in scripture

Special Annual Sabbath (not necessarily falling on the seventh day of a week)

Commemorated event in Israel's history or Israeli national holiday

Event commanded by God to be observed annually

Jehoiachin is released from prison by King Evilmerodach of Babylon, 2 Kings 25:27-30, Jer. 52:31-34. One scripture states this occurred on Adar 25, the other, Adar 27. Most commentaries share the opinion that the 25th was the date of the king's edict for his release, but the 27th was the date the edict was finally carried out.

16 17 18 19 20 21 22 23 24 25 26 27 28 29

The Blood Libel declared to be false by Czar Alexander I in 1817 CE. (However, nearly a hundred years later in 1913, this false accusation was employed once again in Kiev.)

Adar has 29 days, except in leap years, when an "extra" Adar month is added. In those years, Adar I is 30 days long, and Adar II is 29 days long. In leap years, Purim is celebrated during Adar II.

Scriptures using the terms *the twelfth month* or *Adar*

2 Kings 25:27 *King Jehoiachin released from prison by the king of Babylon (context verses 27–30)*

It happened in the thirty-seventh year of the captivity of Jehoiachin king of Judah, **in the twelfth month** בִּשְׁנֵים עָשָׂר חֹדֶשׁ , on the twenty-seventh day of the month, that Evilmerodach king of Babylon, in the year that he began to reign, released Jehoiachin king of Judah out of prison.

1 Chronicles 27:15 *David's civil leader – monthly duty schedule*

The twelfth captain **for the twelfth month** לִשְׁנֵים עָשָׂר הַחֹדֶשׁ was Heldai the Netophathite, of Othniel: and in his division were twenty-four thousand.

Ezra 6:15 *The rebuilding of the temple is completed, as decreed by God and by foreign kings (verses 13–16)*

This house was finished on the third day of the month Adar אֲדָר , which was in the sixth year of the reign of Darius the king.

Esther 3:7,13 *Adar 13 is the date to destroy the Jews, according to the lot (context verses 7–15)*

In the first month, which is the month Nisan, in the twelfth year of King Ahasuerus, they cast Pur, that is, the lot, before Haman from day to day, and from month to month, and chose the **twelfth month** שְׁנֵים עָשָׂר , which is **the month Adar** חֹדֶשׁ אֲדָר ...Letters were sent by couriers into all the king's provinces, to destroy, to kill, and to cause to perish, all Jews, both young and old, little children and women, in one day, even on the thirteenth day **of the twelfth month** לְחֹדֶשׁ שְׁנֵים עָשָׂר, which is **the month Adar** חֹדֶשׁ אֲדָר , and to plunder their possessions.

Esther 8:11-12 *The king's edict permits Jewish self defense on Adar 13 (context verses 8–17)*

In those letters, the king granted the Jews who were in every city to gather themselves together, and to defend their life, to destroy, to kill, and to cause to perish, all the power of the people and province that would assault them, their little ones and women, and to plunder their possessions, on one day in all the provinces of King Ahasuerus, on the thirteenth day **of the twelfth month** לְחֹדֶשׁ שְׁנֵים עָשָׂר , which is **the month Adar** חֹדֶשׁ אֲדָר .

Antique "Megillat Esther" (scroll of Esther) with enameled cover and post

"The King's Goblet" (silver Kiddush cup)

"Hamentashen" – Purim cookies in the shape of Haman's hat

"Gragger" (noisemaker) – used during Purim celebration to "wipe out" the name of Haman

Esther 9:1,15-21 *Victory for the Jewish people; institution of the feast of Purim*

Now in the twelfth month וּבִשְׁנֵים עָשָׂר חֹדֶשׁ, which is **the month Adar** חֹדֶשׁ אֲדָר, on the thirteenth day of the month, when the king's commandment and his decree drew near to be put in execution, on the day that the enemies of the Jews hoped to conquer them, (but it was turned out the opposite happened, that the Jews conquered those who hated them)...   ...The Jews who were in Shushan gathered themselves together on the fourteenth day also **of the month Adar** לְחֹדֶשׁ אֲדָר, and killed three hundred men in Shushan; but they didn't lay their hand on the spoil. The other Jews who were in the king's provinces gathered themselves together, defended their lives, had rest from their enemies, and killed seventy-five thousand of those who hated them; but they didn't lay their hand on the plunder. This was done on the thirteenth day **of the month Adar** לְחֹדֶשׁ אֲדָר; and on the fourteenth day of that month they rested and made it a day of feasting and gladness. But the Jews who were in Shushan assembled together on the thirteenth and on the fourteenth days of the month; and on the fifteenth day of that month, they rested, and made it a day of feasting and gladness. Therefore the Jews of the villages, who live in the unwalled towns, make the fourteenth day **of the month Adar** לְחֹדֶשׁ אֲדָר a day of gladness and feasting, a good day, and a day of sending presents of food to one another. Mordecai wrote these things, and sent letters to all the Jews who were in all the provinces of the king Ahasuerus, both near and far, to enjoin them that they should keep the fourteenth and fifteenth days **of the month Adar** לְחֹדֶשׁ אֲדָר yearly...

Jeremiah 52:31 *Jehoiachin released from prison by the king of Babylon (context verses 31-34)*

It happened in the thirty-seventh year of the captivity of Jehoiachin king of Judah, **in the twelfth month** בִּשְׁנֵים עָשָׂר חֹדֶשׁ, in the twenty-fifth day of the month, that Evilmerodach king of Babylon, in the first year of his reign, released Jehoiachin king of Judah out of prison.

Ezekiel 32:1-3 *God commands Ezekiel to mourn for Pharoah, king of Egypt (context verses 1-16)*

It happened in the twelfth year, **in the twelfth month** בִּשְׁנֵי עָשָׂר חֹדֶשׁ, in the first day of the month, that the word of the LORD came to me, saying, "Son of man, take up a lamentation over Pharaoh king of Egypt, and tell him, 'You were likened to a young lion of the nations: yet you are as a monster in the seas; and you did break forth with your rivers, and troubled the waters with your feet, and fouled their rivers. Thus says Adonai the LORD: I will spread out My net on you with a company of many peoples; and they shall bring you up in My net.'"

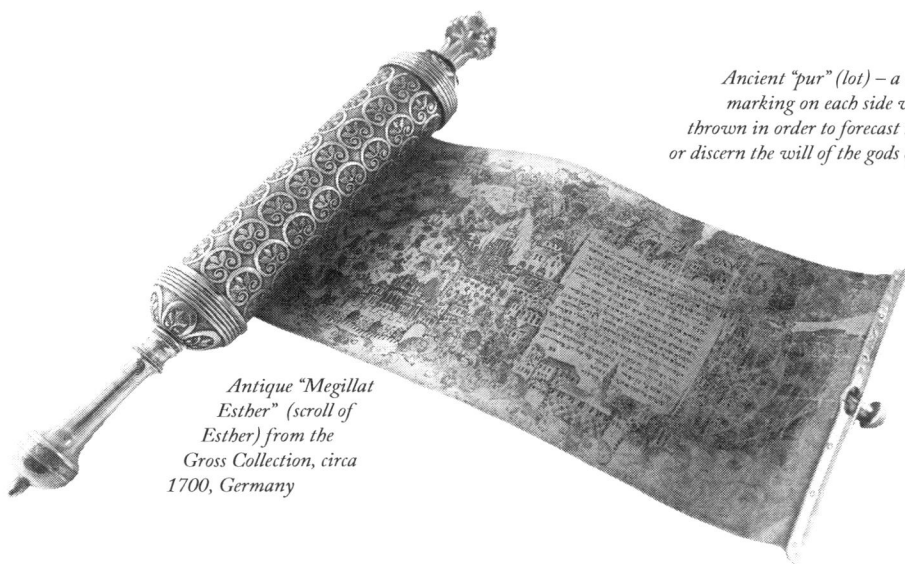

Ancient "pur" (lot) – a cube with marking on each side which was thrown in order to forecast the future or discern the will of the gods of fortune

Antique "Megillat Esther" (scroll of Esther) from the Gross Collection, circa 1700, Germany

"The King's Scepter"

*Thy Word is a lamp unto my feet
and a light unto my path.*

Psalm 119:105

Helpful Resources

You've just finished your study of the month Adar – the twelfth month of the Biblical calendar – which brings us to the conclusion of *Messiah's Calendar Book 1: Days, Weeks, Months and Years.* Before we part, though, we want to give you a few more helpful graphics, articles and a glossary.

May our LORD bless you as you persist in the study of His Holy Word.

Contents

פֶּסַח	חַג הַמַּצּוֹת	יוֹם הַבִּכּוּרִים	חַג שָׁבֻעֹת
PEH-sach	*chag hah-mah-TSŌT*	*yōhm hah-bih-koo-REEM*	*chag shah-voo-ŌT*
Passover	**Unleavened Bread**	**Firstfruits**	**Weeks***
Nisan 14	Nisan 15–21	Nisan 16	Sivan 6
(in the FIRST month)	*(in the FIRST month)*	*(in the FIRST month)*	*(in the THIRD month)*
Leviticus 23:4–5	*Leviticus 23:6–8*	*Leviticus 23:9–14*	*Leviticus 23:15–22* **Greek: "Pentecost" = "fifty"*

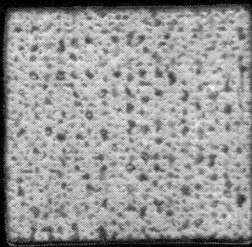

Spring Feasts — Already Fulfilled In Messiah

Messiah's Death	**Messiah's Burial**	**Messiah's Resurrection**	**Indwelling Holy Spirit**
(Deliverance from bondage in Egypt)	(Removal of all leaven / burial of sin)	(Firstfruits: first barley sheaves of the wave offering presented)	(Torah given at Sinai; first wheat sheaves presented)
...for indeed Christ, our Passover, has been sacrificed in our place. *1 Corinthians 5:7* *The next day, [John] saw Jesus coming to him, and said, "Behold, the Lamb of God, who takes away the sin of the world!"* *John 1:29* *...you were redeemed... with precious blood, as of a faultless and pure lamb, the blood of Christ...* *1 Peter 1:18–19*	*Purge out the old leaven, that you may be a new lump, even as you are unleavened...* *1 Corinthians 5:7* *For Him who knew no sin He made to be sin on our behalf; so that in Him we might become the righteousness of God.* *2 Corinthians 5:21*	*But Christ has indeed been raised from the dead, the firstfruits of those who have fallen asleep. For since death came through a man, the resurrection of the dead comes also through a man. For as in Adam all die, so in Christ all will be made alive. But each in turn: Christ, the firstfruits; then, when He comes, those who belong to Him.* *1 Corinthians 15:20–23*	*Now when the day of Pentecost had fully come, they were all with one accord in one place. Suddenly there came from the sky a sound like the rushing of a mighty wind, and it filled all the house where they were sitting. Tongues like fire appeared and were distributed to them, and one sat on each of them. They were all filled with the Holy Spirit...* *Acts 2:1–4*

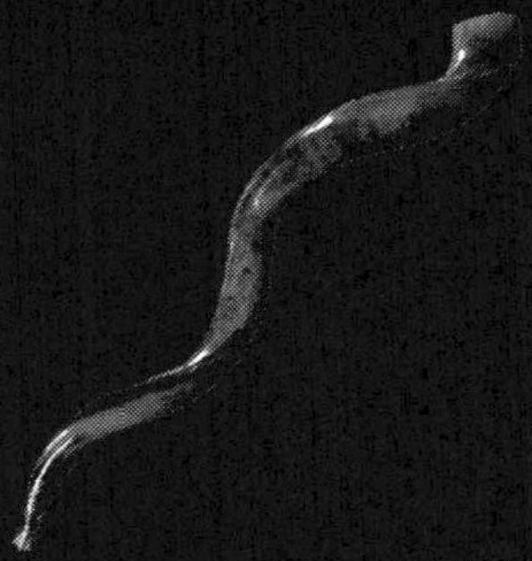

Key:			
Hebrew name of the appointed time	יוֹם תְּרוּעָה	יוֹם כִּפּוּר	סֻכּוֹת
Transliteration (how it is pronounced)	*yōhm t-ROO-ah*	*yōhm kih-POOR*	*soo-KŌT*
English name(s) of the appointed time	Day of Trumpets*	Day of Atonement	Booths* (Tabernacles)
Biblical date(s)	Tishri 1	Tishri 10	Tishri 15-21 plus Eighth Day of Assembly, Tishri 22
Order of month	*(in the SEVENTH month)*	*(in the SEVENTH month)*	*(in the SEVENTH month)*
Mentioned in Leviticus 23	*Leviticus 23:23-25* **Literally, "Day of a shout"*	*Leviticus 23:26-32*	*Leviticus 23:33-34* **Literally, "thicket shelters"*
Past or future fulfillment	*Fall Feasts – Yet To Be Fulfilled*		
New Testament event which this appointed time foreshadows	Translation of Believers	Atonement of all Israel	Millennial Reign
Other significance of this appointed time	("Rapture")	(Israel recognizes Messiah Yeshua)	(Yeshua's 1,000 year earthly reign)
Key New Testament verses describing this appointed time or its symbolic meaning	*For the LORD Himself will descend from heaven with a shout, with the voice of the archangel, and with God's trumpet. The dead in Christ will rise first, then we who are alive, who are left, will be caught up together with them in the clouds, to meet the LORD in the air... 1 Thessalonians 4:16-17* *Behold, I tell you a mystery. We will not all sleep, but we will all be changed, in a moment, in the twinkling of an eye, at the last trumpet. For the trumpet will sound, and the dead will be raised incorruptible, and we will be changed. 1 Corinthians 15:51-52*	*For I don't desire you to be ignorant, brothers, of this mystery, so that you won't be wise in your own conceits, that a partial hardening has happened to Israel, until the fullness of the Gentiles has come in, and so all Israel will be saved. Even as it is written, "There will come out of Zion the Deliverer, and he will turn away ungodliness from Jacob." Romans 11:25-26*	*It will happen that everyone who is left of all the nations that came against Jerusalem will go up from year to year to worship the King, the LORD of Armies, and to keep the feast of tabernacles. It will be, that whoever...doesn't go up to Jerusalem to worship the King, the LORD of Armies, on them there will be no rain. Zechariah 14:16-17* *Now on the last and greatest day of the feast, Jesus stood and cried out, "If anyone is thirsty, let him come to Me and drink! He who believes in Me, as the Scripture has said, from within him will flow rivers of living water." John 7:37-38*

The Biblical Months Song

When we were first introduced to the Biblical calendar, we really struggled to learn the order of the months of the Biblical year. One day, God inspired us with a clever jingle to help us memorize them. This little song lets you sing the post-exilic month names to the well-known tune of "A Partridge In a Pear Tree."

In the ho- ly words of To- rah my Fath-er gave to me the

feasts of Lev-it-icus twenty - three and the 12 months of the Bi - ble He

gave to you and me Nih - san Ih-yar Sih- vahn, Tah- mooz Av Eh ---

lool Tish - ree Chesh - vahn -------- Kis - layv

Tay- vet Sh'- vaht Ah- dar & sometimes A- dar Shay- nee.

The Four Calls of the Shofar
and their
Prophetic Significance

Each "call" of the shofar signifies a specific melody to be played on the ram's horn. Each call has a name.
In a religious service, the worship leader will loudly cry out the call's name, and the person blowing the shofar will
respond, playing the correct melody. The worship leader calls each name in a specific order, as shown below.
This order is traditional, and, as you will see from its symbolism, it carries spiritual significance –
telling the story of God's plan of the ages, from Creation to our final redemption in the Eternal State.

Shofar Call	Meaning of the Call's Hebrew Name	Quality of the Call's Melody	Prophetic Significance
First Call: **TEKIAH** תְּקִיעָה *t'-KEE-ah*	"a blow or blast"	One long, full, uninterrupted blast; a **WHOLE** note	The state of **wholeness** of God's creation (and of mankind) before sin entered the world through Adam
Second Call: **SHEVARIM** שְׁבָרִים *sh'-vah-REEM*	"to destroy, to break into pieces"	Three short, whooping blasts, together lasting as long as one tekiah blast; a **BROKEN** note	Sin's breaking power; the **brokenness** of mankind and of creation as a result of sin entering the world
Third Call: **TERUAH** תְּרוּעָה *t'-ROO-ah*	"shout of joy or alarm, a war cry"	Nine staccato blasts, together lasting as long as one tekiah blast; a **SEVERELY BROKEN** note	The call of alarm (and joy) believers will hear at the translation of our sin-ridden bodies to immortal bodies; also signals a time of **severe brokenness** of unsaved mankind and all creation during the last days
Final Call: **TEKIAH G'DOLAH** תְּקִיעָה גְדוֹלָה *t'-KEE-ah g'-do-LAH*	"a great blast"	One long blast, held out as long as possible, a very long **WHOLE** note	The redemption of all believers' bodies from mortality to immortal wholeness, and the restoration of creation to perfect **wholeness,** with a new heavens and new earth

Rosh Chodesh:
Its History and Liturgy

Since the Biblical calendar is based on the lunar (moon) cycle, the determination of **the first day of the lunar month** *(Rosh Chodesh)* is crucial for observing the Biblical appointed times on the correct days (for those who choose to do so). Abraham Millgram, in the book *Jewish Worship*, describes the manner in which new moons were determined in Biblical times.

> The procedure of fixing the date of the new moon is graphically recorded in the Mishnah (R.H. 2:5-7). On the the thirtieth day of each month the head of the court (Sanhedrin) would examine the witnesses who claimed to have seen the crescent of the new moon. When he was satisfied with the evidence, he would call out, "The new moon is consecrated," and the people assembled in the Temple court would respond: "It is consecrated, it is consecrated." The shofar (ram's horn) was blown, and the festivities, including the Temple rites, would begin.

Some of the traditional liturgy of Rosh Chodesh is included below. Much of it comes from ancient times, and it is still sung today in observant Jewish and Messianic congregations on Rosh Chodesh.

The Scripture Reading for Rosh Chodesh is from Psalm 148:1-6:

> Halleluyah! Praise the LORD from the heavens! Praise Him in the heights! Praise Him, all His angels! Praise Him, all His army! Praise Him, sun and moon! Praise Him, all you shining stars! Praise Him, you heavens of heavens, you waters that are above the heavens. Let them praise the name of the LORD, for He commanded, and they were created. He has also established them forever and ever. He has made a decree which will not pass away.

The B'rachah (Blessing of the LORD) which is sung on Rosh Chodesh:

> Blessed are You, LORD our God, King of the Universe, Whose Word created the heavens, Whose breath created all that they contain (Ps. 33:6). Statutes and seasons He set for them, that they should not deviate from their assigned task. Happily, gladly, they do the will of their Creator, Whose work is dependable. Blessed are You, LORD, Who renews the months.

Greetings are exchanged:

> *Shalom ah-lay-chem.* "Peace be upon you."

> *Ah-lay-chem shalom.* "Upon you be peace."

Glossary and Index

Abib *ah-BEEB* • the pre-exilic name of the first Biblical month. (38, 40, 47)

Adar *ah-DAR* • the post-exilic name of the twelfth Biblical month. In leap years, there are two months of Adar: Adar I (also called *Adar Aleph* or *Adar Rishon*) and Adar II (also called *Adar Bet* or *Adar Sheni.*) (39, 41, 119)

appointed time • in Biblical terminology, a day or period of days which God designates for His own specific, holy purposes. See also **moadim** (42-43, 126-127)

Av *ahv* • the post-exilic name of the fifth Biblical month. (39, 40, 75)

BCE • "before common era" – a synonym for BC ("before Christ"). Also abbreviated *B.C.E., b.c.e.* or *bce.* This term is used in scientific and academic publications which must maintain a neutral position with regard to religious beliefs. Also commonly used in Jewish publications. See also **CE**.

Biblical calendar • The calendar system devised by God in scripture, which begins its year with the month Nisan. (40, 44)

Booths, Feast of • see **Sukkot.**

Bul *bool* • the pre-exilic name of the eighth Biblical month. (38, 41, 95)

CE • "common era" – a synonym for AD ("Anno Domini," *Latin,* "in the year of the Lord"). Also abbreviated *C.E., c.e.* or *ce.* This term is used in scientific and academic publications which must maintain a neutral position with regard to religious beliefs. Also commonly used in Jewish publications. See also **BCE**.

Chag Ha Matzah *chag ha-mah-tsah* • a term transliterated from Hebrew meaning "feast of unleavened bread." In the Hebrew scriptures, called Chag Ha Matsot (*chag ha-mah-tsōt.*) See also **Unleavened Bread.** (43, 47, 126)

Chanukah *chah-noo-kah* • a term transliterated from Hebrew meaning "dedication." A man-made feast celebrating the miraculous deliverance, cleansing and rededicating of the temple after the abomination of desolation during Maccabean period. A spiritual type of the destruction of the coming antichrist. (101)

Cheshvan or Marcheshvan *chesh-VAHN, mar-chesh-VAHN* • the post-exilic name of the eighth Biblical month. (39, 41, 95)

Chodesh *CHŌ-desh* • a word transliterated from Hebrew meaning "month." From the Hebrew root *chadash,* meaning "to renew, to repair." (33, 130)

civil calendar • a calendar (in any country) which is used within that country for civil, official or administrative purposes. See also **Jewish civil calendar.**

Day of Atonement • see **Yom Kippur.**

Glossary and Index

Days of Awe • the ten days between Tishri 1 (Feast of Trumpets) and Tishri 10 (Day of Atonement) during which traditional Jews repent of their sins of the past year. (88)

ecclesiastical calendar • see **religious calendar.**

Eighth Day of Assembly • see **Shemini Atzeret.**

Elul *eh-LOOL* • the post-exilic name of the sixth Biblical month. (39, 40, 81)

equinox • the time or date (twice each year) when day and night are of equal length (around September 22 and March 20).

Etanim *ay-tah-NEEM* • the pre-exilic name of the seventh Biblical month. (38, 41, 87)

"Fast, The" • "The Fast" is the fast day of **Yom Kippur**, the Day of Atonement, the only fast commanded by God in scripture. (88, 127)

Fast of Gedaliah • a man-made fast held on Tishri 3, commemorating the assassination of Gedaliah, a governor of Judah. Also called the **Fast of the Seventh Month.** (87, 88)

Fast of the Fifth Month • a man-made fast held on the **Ninth of Av.** (75, 76)

Fast of the Fourth Month • "Shivah Asar b'Tammuz," the "Fast of the 17th of Tammuz," a man-made fast commemorating the Five Tragedies of Tammuz 17. (69, 71)

Fast of the Seventh Month • Also called the "Fast of Gedaliah," a man-made fast held on Tishri 3, commemorating the assassination of Gedaliah, a governor of Judah. (87, 88)

Fast of the Tenth Month • *Asara b'Tevet* in Hebrew – a man-made fast held on the tenth day of Tevet, mourning the day Nebuchadnezzar began his siege of Jerusalem. (107, 108)

Firstfruits, Feast of • a feast of the Lord held Nisan 16. Hebrew, **Yom Ha Bikkurim**. Jesus was resurrected on this date. (43, 47, 126)

Gregorian calendar • also called the "western calendar." The calendar currently used in America, Europe and western society, containing the months January, February, etc. So named for Pope Gregory XIII, who decreed its use in 1582 CE. This calendar is a modification of the earlier Julian calendar, which was decreed in 46 BCE by Julius Caesar. (15)

holy convocation • a day or other time period designated by God for a holy, formal assembly of the people.

intercalary *inter-CAL-ah-ree* or *in-TER-kuh-layr-ee* • a day or a month which is inserted into the calendar to make it align with the solar year or some other agricultural or astronomical annual occurrence. In the western calendar, February 29 is an *intercalary* day, added in leap years. In the Biblical calendar, Adar II is an *intercalary* month, added in leap years.

Glossary and Index

Iyar *ee-YAR* • the post-exilic name of the second Biblical month. (39, 40, 57)

Jewish civil calendar • a civil calendar developed by Jewish people (in ancient Israel, but also continuing in the Diaspora) for the purpose of keeping track of planting, harvesting and land leases. The Jewish civil calendar begins its year with the month Tishri.

jubilee year • a special sabbath year following seven regular sabbath years, occurring every fifty years. A year of rest for the land and a time that everyone is to return to his own property. (45)

Kislev *kiss-lev* • the post-exilic name of the ninth Biblical month. (39, 41, 101)

lunar calendar • a calendar in which the first day of every month is determined by the cycle of the moon.

Marcheshvan • see **Cheshvan**.

Messianic believer • a Jewish person who believes in Jesus (Hebrew, *Yeshua*) as Messiah and LORD, who has received His free gift of salvation by grace through faith (and not by works), and who chooses to continue to embrace those elements of his or her Jewish culture which are Biblical, such as God's calendar. Also, the term "Messianic" may apply to a Gentile who chooses to participate in this particular style of Biblical worship. "Messianic congregations" are comprised of born-again Jews and Gentiles who choose to join together in a Messianic style of worship.

moadim *mo-ah-DEEM* • a word transliterated from Hebrew, meaning "appointed times." (42-43, 126-127)

new moon • the phase of the moon when it first becomes visible as a slender crescent (as defined by ancient Judaism for religious purposes. For the modern astronomical definition, see **waxing crescent**). The presence of the new moon signals the beginning of the Biblical month. See also **Rosh Chodesh.** (34-37)

Ninth of Av • termed the "saddest day in Jewish history," the date of the destruction of both the first and the second temples, as well as other national tragedies. A man-made fast day, also called the **Fast of the Fifth Month.** (75, 76)

Nisan *nee-SAHN* • the post-exilic name of the first Biblical month. (39, 40, 47)

Passover • see **Pesach**.

Pentecost • see **Weeks, Feast of**.

Pesach *PEH-sach* • a word transliterated from Hebrew, meaning "Passover." Held on Nisan 14, this is also the date of Jesus' crucifixion (43, 47, 126)

pre-exilic • literally, "before the exile." In the case of Israel, this refers to the time period before Israel was exiled to Babylon. Pre-exilic Biblical month names came from the Canaanite culture and language.

Glossary and Index

post-exilic • literally, "after the exile." In the case of Israel, this refers to the time period after Israel's exile in Babylon. Post-exilic Biblical month names came from the Babylonian culture and language.

Purim *poo-REEM* • a word transliterated from Hebrew, meaning "lots." The name of a man-made feast held in the month Adar, celebrating God's miraculous deliverance of the Jewish people as described in the book of Esther. (119, 120)

religious calendar • a calendar whose purpose is to keep track of religious observances. Also called an "ecclesiastical calendar." The Jewish religious calendar, with the exception of some additional man-made fast days and a few minor feast days, is otherwise identical to God's Biblical calendar, which begins its year with the month Nisan.

Rosh Chodesh *rōsh CHŌ-desh* • a term transliterated from Hebrew, meaning "head of the month." The first day of the Biblical month. See also **new moon**. (33-37, 130)

Rosh HaShanah *rōsh hah-shah-NAH* • a term transliterated from Hebrew, meaning "head of the year." The first day of the Jewish civil year, which is Tishri 1. See also **Yom Teruah**. (87)

sabbath • a day or other time period designated by God as a day of rest, on which no regular work is to be done. May additionally be designated as a **holy convocation.** (26-31)

sabbath year • a year in which the land is allowed to rest; fields are not to be sown, vineyards are not to be pruned. The sabbath year occurs every seventh year. (45)

Shavuot *sha-voo-ŌT* • a word transliterated from Hebrew, meaning "weeks." An appointed time of the LORD held on Sivan 6, exactly fifty days following Firstfruits, from which is derived its Greek name, *Pentecost*, meaning "fifty." See also **Weeks, Feast of.** (43, 63, 126)

Shemini Atzeret *sh'mee-NEE ah-TSAYR-et* • a term transliterated from Hebrew, meaning "eighth day of assembly," the last great day of the Feast of Tabernacles. (89)

Shevat *sh'-VAHT* • the post-exilic name of the eleventh Biblical month. (39, 41, 113)

shofar *shō-FAR* • a word transliterated from Hebrew, meaning a ram's horn which is hollowed out for use as a trumpet in Biblical religious observances or to announce the **new moon.** Also once used in ancient Israel as a battle signal or alarm. (129)

Simchat Torah *sim-chat to-RAH* • a term transliterated from Hebrew, meaning "rejoicing in the Torah," held on the last great day of the Feast of Tabernacles, a joyful celebration of reading the Torah scroll and rolling it back to its beginning place at Genesis 1:1 (89)

Sivan *see-VAHN* • the post-exilic name of the third Biblical month. (39, 40, 63)

Glossary and Index

solar calendar • a calendar in which the first day of each year is determined by the cycle of the sun, and the months are determined by dividing up the year into predetermined segments, without regard for the lunar cycle.

solstice • either of the two times in the year (*summer solstice* or *winter solstice*) when the sun is farthest north or south of the equator, resulting in the longest and shortest days of the year (around June 21 and December 22).

Sukkot *soo-KŌT* • a word transliterated from Hebrew, meaning "booths" or "tabernacles." A seven-day feast of the LORD held Tishri 15-21 followed by an additional eighth day of assembly on Tishri 22. A symbolic type of the coming thousand-year reign of Jesus, in which peace and prosperity will flow worldwide. Jesus made His famous statement that He was the source of living water on the last great day (eighth day) of this feast. (43, 87, 127)

Ta'anit Esther • the "Fast of Esther," a minor man-made fast from dawn until dusk on Purim eve, commemorating the three-day fast observed by the Jewish people in the book of Esther. (120)

Tabernacles, Feast of • see **Sukkot.**

Tammuz *tah-MOOZ* • the post-exilic name of the fourth Biblical month. (39, 40, 69)

Tevet *tay-VAYT* • the post-exilic name of the tenth Biblical month. (39, 41, 107)

Three Weeks of Sorrow • a period of mourning held by observant Jews beginning with the man-made Fast of Tammuz and culminating in the man-made fast of the Ninth of Av. (69, 71, 76)

Tishri or Tishrei *tish-ree* or *tish-ray* • the post-exilic name of the seventh Biblical month. (39, 41, 87)

transliteration • a method of writing the pronunciation of a foreign word using the letters of one's own alphabet. For example, the Hebrew word שָׁלוֹם may be *transliterated* as "shalom."

Trumpets, Feast of • see **Yom Teruah.**

Tu b'Shevat *too b'-sh'-VAHT* • the 15th day of the month Shevat, a day ordained by the rabbis for calculating the beginning of the agricultural cycle. Israeli "Arbor Day." (113, 114)

Unleavened Bread, Feast of • a seven-day feast of the LORD held Nisan 15-21. Hebrew, *Chag Ha Matzah.* Jesus was in the grave during this feast. (Also used interchangeably with the term "Passover" as shorthand to refer to the *general* time period in which all three appointed times of Nisan occur: *Passover, Unleavened Bread,* and *Firstfruits.*) (43, 47, 126)

Glossary and Index

waxing crescent • according to modern astronomy, the first appearance of a slender crescent *after* the phase of the new moon, which is itself invisible. It was the *waxing crescent* which the ancient Israelites actually looked for to determine if a new moon had indeed occurred. (33)

Weeks, Feast of • An appointed time of the LORD held on Sivan 6, exactly fifty days following Firstfruits (from which is derived its Greek name, *Pentecost*, "fifty"). Moses received the Torah on Mount Sinai (according to tradition) on this date. The believers of Acts chapter 2 received the indwelling Holy Spirit on this date. See also **Shavuot.** (43, 63, 126)

western calendar • See **Gregorian calendar.**

Yeshua *yay-SHOO-ah* • an Old Testament Hebrew name (Jeshua), a short form of *y'ho-SHOO-ah* (Joshua), meaning "the LORD is salvation." Greek, Ἰησοῦς *Ee-ay-sooss*, English, *Jesus. Yeshua* was the name that the first-century disciples of Jesus (and His earthly family members) used when speaking to Him.

Yom Ha Bikkurim *yom hah bih-koo-REEM* • a term transliterated from Hebrew, meaning "day of firstfruits." An appointed time of the LORD held on Nisan 16. Jesus was resurrected on this date. See also **Firstfruits, Feast of.** (43, 47, 126)

Yom Kippur *yom kih-POOR* • a term transliterated from Hebrew, meaning "the "day of atonement." Called "Yom Ha Kippurim" *(yom ha-kih-poo-REEM)* in scripture. An appointed time of the LORD held on Tishri 10, the most holy day of the Biblical year and the only fast day in all of scripture commanded by God. A prophetic type of the future atonement of all Israel. (43, 87, 88, 126)

Yom Teruah *yom t'-ROO-ah* • a term transliterated from Hebrew, meaning "day of a shout," and by extension, "day of a blast" (of a trumpet). Commonly termed "The Feast of Trumpets," an appointed time of the LORD held on Tishri 1. A prophetic type of the future translation of believers, also called "the Rapture." (43, 87, 88, 127)

Ziv *zihv* • the pre-exilic name of the second Biblical month. (38, 40, 57)

Other Books
by James T. and Lisa M. Cummins

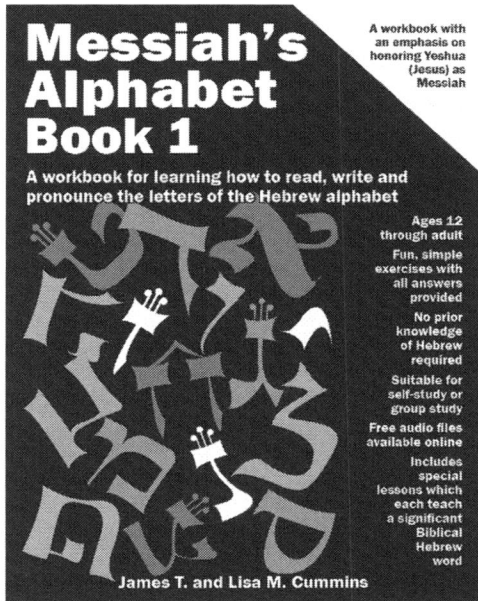

Messiah's Alphabet Book 1: A workbook for learning how to read, write and pronounce the letters of the Hebrew alphabet

The first book in the *Messiah's Alphabet* series introduces the Hebrew alphabet to those with no prior knowledge of Hebrew. The student is shown how to draw simple "stick figure" shapes for each letter, and then learns the sound and name of each letter in a fun and friendly manner. The book gradually introduces some of the most frequently used Hebrew words in the Bible, gently assisting the reader in learning to recognize and pronounce each one. Audio files of every lesson available.

Available now through online book retailers

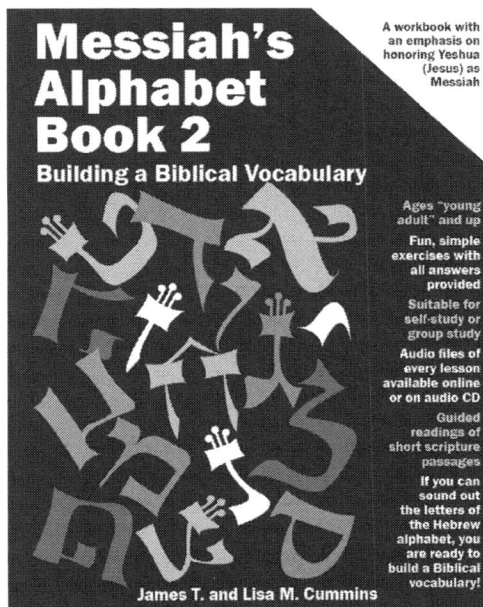

Messiah's Alphabet Book 2:
Building a Biblical Vocabulary

The second book in the *Messiah's Alphabet* series, this workbook teaches basic Hebrew grammar on topics such as the definite article "the", the conjunction "and," plural nouns, adjectives and possessives for singular nouns. Guided readings of short scripture passages are included throughout. Fun, simple exercises with all answers are provided. Puzzles, riddles and tear-out "flashcard" pages are included. Intended for students who have completed Book 1 or who have a solid working knowledge of the Hebrew alphabet and are able to phonetically "sound out" Hebrew words. Audio files of every lesson available.

Available now through online book retailers

Other Books by James T. and Lisa M. Cummins, *continued*

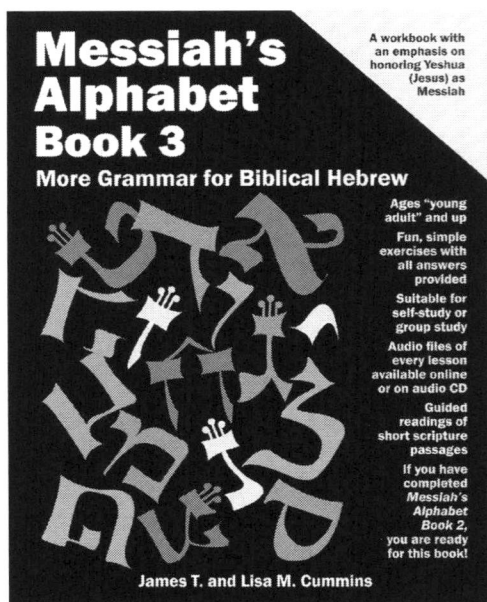

Messiah's Alphabet Book 3
More Grammar for Biblical Hebrew

A workbook with an emphasis on honoring Yeshua (Jesus) as Messiah

Ages "young adult" and up

Fun, simple exercises with all answers provided

Suitable for self-study or group study

Audio files of every lesson available online or on audio CD

Guided readings of short scripture passages

If you have completed *Messiah's Alphabet Book 2*, you are ready for this book!

James T. and Lisa M. Cummins

Messiah's Alphabet Book 3: More Grammar for Biblical Hebrew
The third book in the *Messiah's Alphabet* series covers topics such as participles, prepositions (standalone and inseparable), prepositions with pronominal suffixes, and construct chains (word pairs). Each lesson introduces plenty of new Biblical Hebrew vocabulary. Continuing in the same fun and friendly style as the other books in the series, the workbook contains cartoons, jokes, puzzles, flashcard pages, and answers to all exercises. Audio files of vocabulary from every lesson are available.

Available now through online book retailers

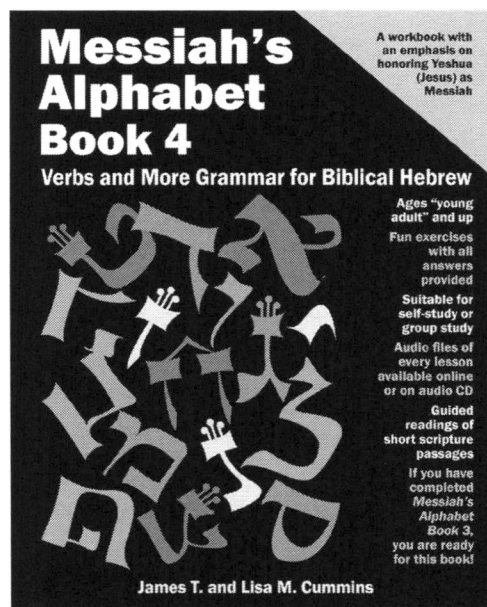

Messiah's Alphabet Book 4
Verbs and More Grammar for Biblical Hebrew

A workbook with an emphasis on honoring Yeshua (Jesus) as Messiah

Ages "young adult" and up

Fun exercises with all answers provided

Suitable for self-study or group study

Audio files of every lesson available online or on audio CD

Guided readings of short scripture passages

If you have completed *Messiah's Alphabet Book 3*, you are ready for this book!

James T. and Lisa M. Cummins

Messiah's Alphabet Book 4: Verbs and More Grammar for Biblical Hebrew
The fourth book in the *Messiah's Alphabet* series covers verbs (roots, past tense, future tense, imperative and infinitive), the direct object marker, possessive suffixes for plural nouns, and the reversing *vav*. Each lesson introduces new Biblical Hebrew vocabulary. Continuing in the same fun and friendly style as the other books in the series, the workbook contains cartoons, jokes, puzzles, flashcard pages, and answers to all exercises. The book also includes Verb Charts, which give conjugations of frequently used verbs. Audio files of all newly introduced vocabulary are available.

Available now through online book retailers

Other Books by James T. and Lisa M. Cummins, *continued*

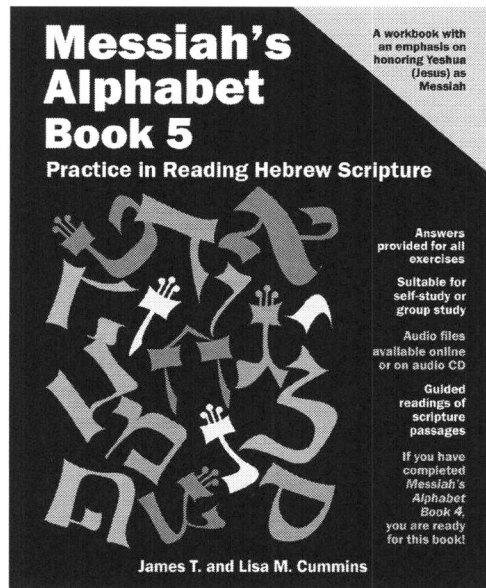

Messiah's Alphabet Book 5

Practice in Reading Hebrew Scripture

A workbook with an emphasis on honoring Yeshua (Jesus) as Messiah

Answers provided for all exercises

Suitable for self-study or group study

Audio files available online or on audio CD

Guided readings of scripture passages

If you have completed *Messiah's Alphabet Book 4,* you are ready for this book!

James T. and Lisa M. Cummins

Messiah's Alphabet Book 5: Practice in Reading Hebrew Scripture allows the student who has completed Books 1 through 4 of the series to spread his or her wings and practice reading entire passages of scripture, using mostly the vocabulary already taught in the series. Some new vocabulary is taught in this book, too, including tear-out flashcard pages, verb charts and glossary. Comparison tables of Christian, traditional Jewish and Messianic translations for every passage are included. Intriguing discussion questions explore selected Hebrew phrases. Complete answer keys with grammatical notations included. Emphasis on Yeshua (Jesus) as Savior and LORD. Audio files of every lesson available.

Available now through online book retailers

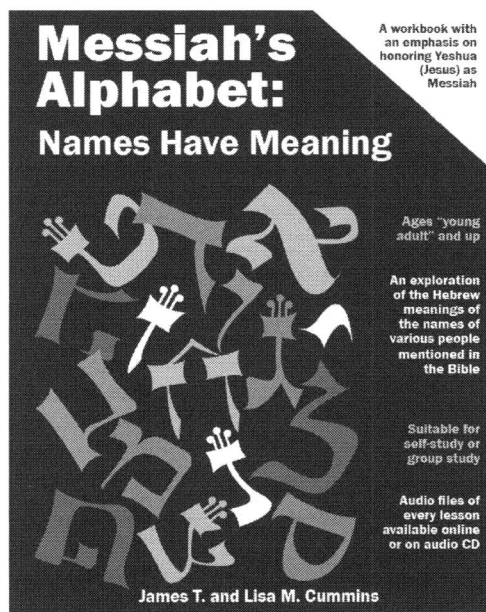

Messiah's Alphabet:

Names Have Meaning

A workbook with an emphasis on honoring Yeshua (Jesus) as Messiah

Ages "young adult" and up

An exploration of the Hebrew meanings of the names of various people mentioned in the Bible

Suitable for self-study or group study

Audio files of every lesson available online or on audio CD

James T. and Lisa M. Cummins

Messiah's Alphabet: Names Have Meaning is an exploration into the actual Hebrew meanings of the names of certain people mentioned in the Bible. Surprising discoveries will unfold as you connect the true meaning of each Hebrew name with its prophetic significance and fulfillment in scripture. The hidden Hebrew meanings underlying the names of New Testament people will also be brought to light. While a basic knowledge of the Hebrew and Greek alphabets may be helpful, it is not necessary, as all pronunciations are provided in transliteration form using the standard alphabet of English. All answers are provided in the text. Audio files of every lesson available.

Available now through online book retailers

Other Books by James T. and Lisa M. Cummins, *continued*

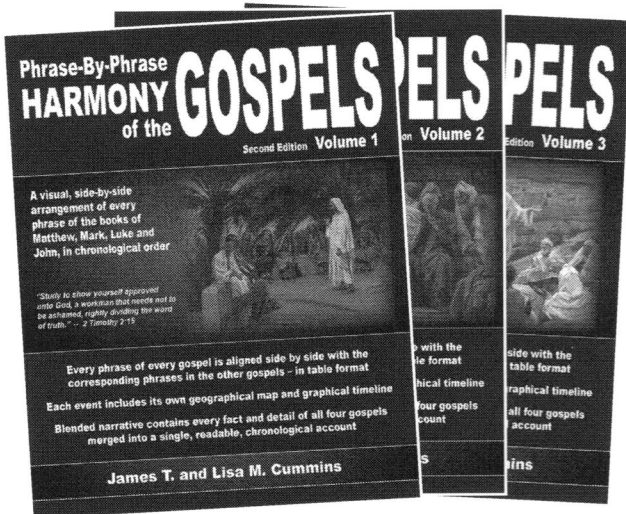

Phrase-By-Phrase Harmony of the Gospels – This is a visual, side-by-side arrangement of every phrase of the books of Matthew, Mark, Luke and John, in chronological order. Every phrase of every gospel is aligned side by side with the corresponding phrases in the other gospels, in table format. Each event includes its own geographical map and graphical timeline. Blended narrative contains every fact and detail of all four gospels, merged into a single, readable, chronological account.

Available now through online book retailers

Modular design: Focus your attention on one event per section.

Graphical Timeline on every section: Keep track of what happened before and what's coming up.

Phrase-By-Phrase Harmonized Table: Compare every phrase of scripture from all four gospels at a glance. Bolded and italicized typefaces indicate time and geography references.

SECTION 17 — Christ's baptism in the river Jordan

Graphical Timeline

16 silent years

| 15 Jesus at age 12 goes up to the Passover | 16 Preparatory preaching of John the baptizer | 17 Christ's baptism in the river Jordan | 18 Spirit leads Jesus into wilderness; Satan tempts Jesus | 19 John the baptizer's witness to Jesus as the Messiah |

Chronological Notes:
Mk 1:9 "in those days" follows immediately after the passage speaking of John the baptizer's preparatory preaching and baptizing ministry, indicating that Jesus came to John during that same span of John's ministry. "In those days" is also a phrase having spiritual significance in the Hebrew scriptures as denoting a period of revelation or miracles.
Lk 3:21 "when all the people were baptized"... "Jesus also being baptized" connotes the same time span for both events.

Geography

Nazareth of Galilee

Jordan River

PALESTINE AT THE TIME OF JESUS

Geographical Notes:
Mt 3:13 Jesus went from Galilee to Jordan
Mk 1:9 Jesus went from Nazareth of Galilee to Jordan

Phrase-By-Phrase Harmonized Table

Matthew 3: 13-17	Mark 1: 9-11	Luke 3: 21-22	John
	9a And it came to pass *in those days,*	21a Now *when all the people were baptized,* it came to pass,	
13a Then cometh Jesus from __Galilee__	9b that Jesus came from __Nazareth of Galilee.__		
13b to __Jordan__ unto John, to be baptized of him.			
14 But John forbad him, saying, I have need to be baptized of thee, and comest thou to me?			
15a And Jesus answering said unto him, Suffer it to be so now: for thus it becometh us to fulfil all righteousness.			
15b Then he suffered him.			
16a And Jesus, when he was baptized,	9c and was baptized of John in __Jordan.__	21a that Jesus also being baptized,	
16b went up straightway out of the water:	10a and straightway coming up out of the water,		
		21b and praying,	
16c and, lo, the heavens were opened unto him,	10b he saw the heavens opened,	21c the heaven was opened.	
16d he saw the Spirit of God descending like a dove, and lighting upon him:	10c and the Spirit like a dove descending upon him:	22a And the Holy Ghost descended in a bodily shape like a dove upon him.	
17 And lo a voice from heaven, saying, This is my beloved Son, in whom I am well pleased.	11 And there came a voice from heaven, saying, Thou art my beloved Son, in whom I am well pleased.	22b and a voice from heaven, which said, Thou art my beloved Son; in thee I am well pleased.	

Blended Narrative

In those days, when all the people were being baptized by John, Jesus came from Nazareth of Galilee to Jordan to be baptized by John. But John tried to prevent Him, saying, "I need to be baptized by you, and you come to me?" Jesus answered him, "Permit it for now, for in this way it is fitting for us to fulfill all righteousness." Then he permitted Him. When Jesus was baptized by John in the Jordan, He came straightway up out of the water, and praying, he saw the heavens opened to him, and saw the Holy Spirit of God descending in a bodily shape like a dove and landing on Him. And there came a voice from heaven, saying, "You are my beloved Son; in you I am well pleased. This is my beloved Son, in whom I am well pleased."

(Here it is possible that God spoke both to Jesus and to those gathered at the Jordan at the same time, which accounts for the different modes of address – 2nd person singular speaks directly to Jesus, while 3rd person singular speaks about Jesus, as an audible witness to those present.)

In the table above, **bold italic** print indicates a time/chronological reference; **bold underline** print indicates a place/geographical reference.

51

Chronological Notes: Insightful commentary on the historical or cultural significance of all time references.

Geographical Notes with Map on every section: Keep track of where each event occurs. Historical and archaeological notes are provided wherever applicable.

Blended Narrative: This account, in readable modern language, contains every factual detail of all four gospels, in chronological order.

Authors' Commentary is provided wherever clarification of difficult or problematic texts is necessary.

Printed in Great Britain
by Amazon